Vincent Van Duysen

Complete Works

Foreword by Ilse Crawford

Introduction by Marc Dubois

Vincent Van Duysen © 2010 Vincent Van Duysen
Foreword © 2010 Ilse Crawford
Introduction © 2010 Marc Dubois

Designed by Studio Luc Derycke, Ghent

Flemish texts translated by Rebekah Wilson

All Rights Reserved. No part of this publication may be reproduced or transmitted in any form or by any means, electronic or mechanical, including photocopy, recording or any other information storage and retrieval system, without prior permission in writing from the publisher.

First published in 2010 in hardcover in the United States of America by Thames & Hudson Inc., 500 Fifth Avenue, New York, New York 10110

thamesandhudsonusa.com

Reprinted 2015

Library of Congress Catalog Card Number 2009935640

ISBN 978-0-500-34261-9

Printed and bound in China by Toppan Leefung Printing Ltd

Alberto Piovano Photo essay	i
Ilse Crawford Material Man	4
Marc Dubois 'Nobilis Simplicitas'	8
Projects 1993 to the present	22

VVD Residence I	24		Brasserie National	136
AK Residence	28		Cascade Chandelier	
A Silent Sophistication	33		for *Swarovski*	142
Natan Shop	36		VDD Residence	144
DB-VD Residence	40		VVD Residence II	154
M Residence	42		Desk and Chair for *Bulo*	170
VH Residence	48		VDE-L Residence	172
V Residence	54		Pottery Tableware	
Less is More?	59		for *When Objects Work*	178
Sportmax Shop	64		Tile Kitchen for *Obumex*	180
RH-BH Residence	68		DJ-JVD Residence	182
Wash Basin			Journey up the Hill	191
for *Obumex*	74		Window Coat Rack	
Fashion Club	76		for *Viccarbe*	194
Concordia Offices	80		B Residence	196
VL Residence	90		Green Ribbon Light Fixture	
DC Residence	94		for *DAB*	204
M-VS Residence	108		Private Residence	206
Maximalist Austerity	115		Gaston Chair	
Capco Offices	120		for *Poliform*	218
Copyright Bookshop	124		VDV-G Residence	220
VVD Collection			S Residential Complex	234
for *B&B Italia*	130		Neutra Outdoor Collection	
DR Residence	132		for *Tribù*	242

Chronology	244
Resources	270

IC Residence, London, 2001–2002

Ilse Crawford

Material Man

For nine years (1989 to 1998) I edited *Elle Decoration* magazine in the UK. Throughout that time, doing shoots or go-sees, I visited more than a thousand interiors and came to realize that so many of the ones that *looked* good in print felt cold and two-dimensional in reality, while the few that *felt* good – tactile, solid, warm and intriguing – were rarely appealing to a modern aesthetic. Even over a decade later, there is still a dearth of spaces that make us feel human, that we can truly experience rather than feel detached from.

While I was on the magazine I started to look into what it was that made us connect to our surroundings, and came to the conclusion that architecture, independent of style, resonated with us as emotional beings by engaging with us physically, through our senses. This was not about being 'touchy-feely', but a question of acknowledging that we experience the world through our bodies. We are a part of nature, not apart from it, and although architecture that orders space aesthetically and philosophically might look beautiful, it does not on its own make places that connect.

When we touch, we feel. Our feet, for example, are one of the most sensitive parts of our bodies (they have as many nerve endings as our genitals); the pressure points on our feet also carry signals directly to the brain. A tactile, high-quality floor, therefore, should be a given in a building designed for human well-being. This sensibility should apply to anything we touch. The materials we use create atmosphere and carry hidden messages, which largely determine the mood of a space and our relationship to it. This is far from being a new idea. Frederick Nietzsche observed, 'All evidence of truth comes only through the senses.'

But while I could find historical examples of Modernist architects working in this way (Alvar Aalto, Bernard Rudofsky, Lina Bo Bardi) I struggled to find many contemporaries. A really good floor, with life and soul, was a rare thing indeed. Perfect, easy-maintenance finishes were the rule of the day. Then I came across some pictures of work by a young Belgian architect, Vincent Van Duysen. His own place at the time was a conversion of an old Antwerp apartment (p. 24), and it included such traditional elements as oak floors, painted brick, linen half-curtains, and classic upholstery in a crisp, modern plan. The kitchen was a graphic version of the vernacular hearth. And he had a pantry.

VVD Residence I, Antwerp, 1993

It was miles away from the fitted kitchen. So Van Duysen's apartment not only looked good, it was functional and felt good, too. Here was a designer with a sound grasp of materiality, someone who could take materials that were not in the lexicon of 'modern' and make them new, while at the same time creating a modern that was warm and muscular. I met Van Duysen in Antwerp and published several of his projects in the magazine. In the process, we became friends.

In the mid-1990s, Van Duysen was early in his career and had done a number of residential conversions and new houses in and around Antwerp, plus several store interiors, including the Copyright Bookshop (p. 124) and the Simple D'Anvers boutique. Energetic, expressive and passionate about his vocation, Van Duysen has moved way beyond Antwerp since then, although the city remains his base. These days his work can be found in New York and London, Milan and Dubai – even in my own apartment, which I asked him to design a decade ago. His portfolio has expanded considerably to include offices, apartment blocks and large-scale retail spaces, but he still loves to do residential projects. The essential principles remain the same, however, whatever the genre.

In all his architecture and interiors, refined modern proportions are made physical with the contrasting use of modern and traditional materials. From the beginning, Van Duysen has maintained that he never disconnects the concept from the execution; not for him the ordering of a floor from a square-centimetre sample in a catalogue. Instead, he prefers to deal with people who have a traditional knowledge of how to select, finish and fit materials. Belgium still has skilled craftsmen, but these are not 'yes men' on the end of a telephone. Where Van Duysen differs from many of his peers is that he is prepared to develop long-term and time-consuming relationships with these craftsmen, and consequently can arrive at a high level of finish. He is also adept at handling the details that inevitably arise when two materials meet, and when the man-made meets the machine-made. Perhaps some of this attitude can be attributed to his interest in fashion, which has a far more catholic approach to the skills required to achieve its vision than most contemporary design.

When walking around Van Duysen's house in Antwerp, it is clear that the succession of materials is deftly handled: the Belgian bluestone of the kitchen floor, the glossy walls, the wide-planked oak floors, the marble bath; the juxtaposition of the architectural with the irregular; the light and shade. The flow seems effortless. By the end you are not just impressed by the beauty of the spaces, but also by the memory of the details and the feeling of the materials, and it is the latter that stays with you. Van Duysen takes this philosophy through to his new builds. In a residential project in central Antwerp (p. 234), he brings the cobbled floor from outside to inside the building, and plays off the grey brick with the black-and-glass exterior. Inside his own flat, he uses darkness and shadow to give depth and texture to the space's enormously wide entrance halls; an illogical but absolutely human gesture that gives the apartment a sense of generosity throughout.

VVD Residence II, Antwerp, 2001–2003

Ilse Crawford Material Man

VVD Residence II, Antwerp, 2001–2003

In his product design, Van Duysen again uses the material as the starting point. With the stacking storage bowls for When Objects Work (p. 178), the smooth earthenware is contrasted with the warm wood of the lids – a practical, emotionally satisfying and visually alluring solution. In his chandelier for Swarovski (p. 142), which I commissioned as part of the Crystal Palace Project, he took the brief of reinventing the chandelier to its ultimate expression. His torrent of crystal unleashes the emotional power of the material while abandoning the iconography of the traditional chandelier.

Vincent Van Duysen is that rare architect who can combine a modern language of form with an intuitive feel for materials. And it is this extremely rare combination that makes his work so unusual and so special.

Marc Dubois

'Nobilis Simplicitas'
In Search of Noble Simplicity

It goes without saying that, for the architects of the future, the years spent at college or university are hugely significant. Having to absorb a vast amount of knowledge in a short space of time from lecturers, published material and their own experiences, they cannot help but be affected by their environment and the prevailing Zeitgeist. All these factors form the basis of the student of architecture's future development. Vincent Van Duysen began his own studies at the Higher Institute of Architecture Sint-Lucas in Ghent in 1980, the year of the Venice Biennale's seminal exhibition 'The Presence of the Past', directed by Paolo Portoghesi, which saw the emergence of the term 'postmodern architecture'. 'La Strada Novissima' in the Corderie dell'Arsenale brought together work from the most diverse architects. Anything and everything was possible!

The project that attracted the most media attention during the first half of the 1980s was undoubtedly Zaha Hadid's design for the Peak Club in Hong Kong, with its wavy lines and lack of tangible materiality. Another architect making an impression around the same time, particularly with his residential designs, was Tadao Ando, whose Koshino House in Ashiya, Japan, was an example of pure spatial composition. Ando's controlled space was in direct contrast to Hadid's noncommittal plastic and 'matter-free' design, and the young Van Duysen was exposed to both extremes before eventually choosing to pursue a path more similar to the one trodden by Ando.

For an architect, the buildings that one grows up with, that one is surrounded by, are also sure to have an impact and to sharpen a particular affinity or sensitivity. Victor Horta's use of glass skylights in his Art Nouveau townhouses was clearly inspired by the Royal Greenhouses at Laeken, designed by Alphonse Balat. Van Duysen, for his part, was hugely influenced by Roosenberg Abbey at Waasmunster, designed by the Benedictine monk Hans van der Laan. Here, van der Laan used his own measurement system to modulate the space in a highly consistent way. Far from delivering cheap and surprising effects, the architecture is concerned with achieving silence and authenticity, and creating a space for meditation in a world of whirling images. The result is a place suited to quiet reflection, reminiscent of Romanesque architecture.

One event that came to the attention of Van Duysen and his contemporaries was the opening of the Comme des Garçons boutique in Paris in 1982. Not only did designer Rei Kawakubo cause a splash with her fashion collection, but the austere, almost empty store was a statement in its own right. The minimal presentation gave customers the feeling of being in a museum or temple, rather than just a shop. Other Japanese fashion houses, such as Kenzo and Issey Miyake, soon followed suit and began to think about 'store architecture'; little by little the idea of consciously designing such public spaces gained credibility. In the 1980s, architects like David Chipperfield in the UK used store architecture to explain their own vision and to showcase their talent.

Van Duysen has often said that if he had not studied architecture, he would certainly have pursued a career in fashion, and so perhaps it is unsurprising that on finishing his studies he moved to Milan. Working with fashion and interior designer Cinzia Ruggeri and Aldo Cibic (one of the founders, together with Michele De Lucchi, of the Memphis group), Van Duysen became convinced that a designer should both express a concept as clearly as possible, and pay attention to every significant detail while the project was being carried out. He decided that an architect should not limit himself to merely providing an overview of the design, but should be fully involved in the development phase, down to the subtlest differences in materials and colours. There could be no question of separating design and implementation, or of not paying full attention to the implementation process.

Although time-consuming, Van Duysen believed that this attention to detail was essential, rather than incidental, to the process. The smallest part should have the same intensity and power as the whole. All too often the significance of details is underestimated, even completely minimalized, because 'detail' is seen as secondary to the big idea. For Van Duysen, as for Mies van der Rohe, the essence is in the detail: the small things should not be overlooked because the intensity of the basic idea should be present even at this level.

The Belgian context

Architects always operate within a certain social context in which the significance and role of the main contractor (the property owner) cannot be underestimated. When considering Belgian architecture of the 20th century, particularly in a broader European context, it becomes obvious that the most significant contributions were made in the private housing sector. People were encouraged to build their own homes, not least by the amount of land made available to them for this purpose. The trend really began in around 1900, with Horta's townhouse designs and Josef Hoffmann's matchless Stoclet House in Brussels. Today, house construction and renovation is still an important market in Belgium, providing the sorts of contracts with which young architects can still make a

Sportmax Shop, Milan, 1999

Marc Dubois 'Nobilis Simplicitas'

name for themselves. Van Duysen himself did not start with large government commissions, but small residential and retail projects.

The relationship between the architect and the client is different if it is a private home, rather than a public building, that is being built. Van Duysen speaks of 'tailor-made' homes, private spaces designed with the client's complete comfort in mind. With such a high level of involvement on the client's part, it is extremely important that the architect gains a full understanding of his wishes, no matter how difficult they may be to express. The architect needs to be able to understand how the client thinks, and turn him into an enthusiastic participant, rather than just a customer. The words 'owner' and 'client' are often used interchangeably, but for Van Duysen the difference is crucial. Involvement is essential if one is to achieve a good result at the end of the construction process; it means the project is more than just an order. On the other hand, houses do tend to outlast their owners. Most designers, therefore, will be aware of the need to manage overly specific personal tastes.

In Belgium, the way in which building companies are set up tends to reflect the preponderance of these types of smaller contracts. It is not unusual for such companies to use small, highly specialized contractors to achieve the desired result. Van Duysen arrives at his own exacting standard of finish through a combination of the use of highly motivated professionals and relentless monitoring of each project by himself and his team members. High standards demand a high budget, but the architect is helping to sustain technical mastery through his work. Van Duysen believes in taking precise measurements, rather than relying on the silicone gun to cover up mistakes. He is also interested in another, oft-overlooked aspect of the construction phase: that architects can give labourers the opportunity to create something meaningful of which they can be proud. After all, there is a big difference between producing quality work and just doing a job. Let's not forget that, even after the introduction of new techniques and materials, the building process is still highly skilled and labour-intensive in comparison with other manufacturing industries. Buildings are often unique, simply because of the many specific conditions attached to them.

The pursuit of the monolithic form is a popular preoccupation in modern-day architecture. In one of Van Duysen's earliest works, a house in Sint-Amandsberg (p. 40), we can already see how he is striving to achieve a sense of unity. The large, brick construction is reminiscent of an old-fashioned kiln. Its butterfly roof is a variation on the more traditional gable roof, and was subject to administrative opposition before finally being approved. This roof type was first used by Jørn Utzon in 1956 for the Kingohusene residential project at Helsingør, in Denmark. The Sint-Amandsberg house is an example of how the careful positioning of internal walls can produce an interesting interior. Or, as Luis Barragán demonstrated, of how walls are essential for creating spaces. Mastery of this subtle skill is a prerequisite for any architect.

DB-VD Residence, Sint-Amandsberg, 1994–1997

DC Residence, Waasmunster, 1998–2001

The DC Residence in Waasmunster (p. 94) is undoubtedly Van Duysen's most interesting detached house project from the 1990s, introducing as it does a number of space and detail solutions which the architect was to reuse later on. Although the house is situated in a wooded area, the client wanted as much privacy as possible, so Van Duysen designed a high wall around the house to screen the fully glazed dining room from the road. While the front of the house has very few windows, the back is nearly all glass and has a view over the garden. There is a spacious, double-height entrance hall which forms the focal point of the house; at the top of this hall are two large windows, one of which is internal and set at the top of the stairs, the other is external and overlooks an outdoor terrace. The layout creates interesting perspectives throughout the house and takes advantage of orientation. The outdoor terrace lets the sun into the main bedroom in the morning and the entrance hall in the evening. The corridor to the bedrooms also has a large window onto the terrace, and ends with a full-height, full-width window. This window becomes more than just a source of light, it is an intimate nature painting.

This manipulation of space – the high entrance hall with the adjacent terrace on the first floor – gives the house a dimension of openness that goes beyond conventional ideas about voids and partitions. The solution makes optimum use of the orientation of the building site, something which is always of key importance to Van Duysen. The garden is visible upon entering the house, thanks to the use of an open staircase. Every part of the building was designed with the utmost attention to detail, including the living-room furniture, which exists as a self-contained whole within its surroundings. With a nod to the furniture designs of Donald Judd, the pieces fit in well with the overall approach, whereby the vertical surfaces (the walls) constitute the regulating factor within the interior.

Dating from around the same time is the VDD Residence in Dendermonde (p. 144). As with the house in Sint-Amandsberg, the architect opts once again for visible masonry. The overall design is more traditional: on the garden side, the façade is fronted by eight tall pillars, but Van Duysen nevertheless avoids rigid symmetry by making the three openings different sizes. The large expanse of water which stretches the width of the house is more than a swimming pool, it is also a mirror between the house and the garden. Here, too, the space has been developed so as to create long interior views.

With each new project, Van Duysen's predilection for turning brick into a feature in its own right becomes more evident. The most obvious example of this is the VDV-G Residence in Zonhoven (p. 220). In order to achieve a monolithic appearance, Van Duysen opted to use matching brick to face the visible parts of the flat roof and the underside of the corbels and for the garden walls. Inside, the high stairwell forms the focal point of the house, in which two staircases rise to the first floor. The precise location of the interior walls helps to create a sense of flow. In the large living room, the specially designed windows

VDD Residence, Dendermonde, 1998–2003

Marc Dubois 'Nobilis Simplicitas'

have corners that disappear when the windows are open, to create a feeling of continuity between the interior and exterior spaces. Wide hinged and sliding doors give the option to partition the space. This solution – using large doors as sliding walls – has since become almost standard in Van Duysen's residential projects.

The townhouse

The concept of urban living dates back to the Middle Ages, when people first began to build houses next to each other. This practice gave rise to what we know today as the terraced house or townhouse, a vertical building between two closed party walls that opens onto a public right of way at the front and a garden or courtyard at the back. It was Victor Horta who first injected a sense of space into these houses, overriding their rigid internal demarcation. His liberating designs created openness and a sense of continuity where before there had been nothing more than a collection of closed rooms. Like Horta and many other Belgian architects, Van Duysen too has built and renovated several townhouses.

The VH Residence in Lokeren (p. 48) can hardly be seen from the street. After extensive internal renovations, the result was a space in which it is possible to experience both the width and the height of the building at the same time. The living room at the rear of the house is double-height, and the introduction of a large, open space on the first floor gives a diagonal perspective through the house, which increases the visual openness of the interior yet further. The area directly above the open space is glazed, bathing the centre of the house in a suffusion of light, after the fashion of Horta's townhouse designs. Even the built-in cupboards and the lighting have been positioned so as to accentuate the building's lengthwise orientation. At the back of the house, three large windows connect the interior to the garden.

In Antwerp, the RA Residence is built on an extremely narrow plot, but Van Duysen managed to create a huge sense of openness by means of a few clever touches. The whole focus is towards the back of the house and specifically the terrace, which functions as an urban outdoor space. The high windows open and fold back completely, serving to blur the distinction between the inside and the outside. The VDE-L townhouse in Kortrijk (p. 172), designed in collaboration with Pascal Bilquin and Stephanie Laperre, is a completely new building, as can be seen from its simple, clean lines. On the top floor, a narrow outdoor space behind the windowless façade helps to provide privacy for the uppermost rooms, creating a special ambience inside without the loss of all natural light. The staircases leading to the living and sleeping areas are in different places in the house and run in different directions, creating an interesting interior circulation path. Here, too, the design has been driven by the desire for maximum openness in the interior.

VH Residence, Lokeren, 1995–1998

A fascination for staircases and natural stone

One of Van Duysen's favourite houses is in Antwerp's Populierenlaan, designed in 1926 by Le Corbusier for the painter René Guiette. It was the first time Le Corbusier was able to test out his 'Citrohan' model, in which the architect used a straight, continuous staircase to link all the floors to each other. The resulting spatial effect is impressive.

Van Duysen also pays special attention to staircases in his work. Stairs are about more than linking floors, they can be used to get the most out of the space available. The location and the design of staircases are both extremely important factors as far as the interior design is concerned. The model of the straight, continuous staircase can be seen in Van Duysen's JVD Gallery in Brussels. The high stairwell is accentuated even further by the narrow glass panels in the roof above. There is something about high, narrow staircases that makes one want to climb them, or at least so said Le Corbusier in a reference to a Charlie Chaplin film, *The Kid*, which featured a staircase that reaches up to the sky.

Staircases are very important in Van Duysen's other projects, too. In the Natan store in Brussels (p. 36), the space is defined by the staircase. The interior is an equal mix of horizontal and vertical lines, with the only slanting line provided by the closed handrail. The wall opposite to the handrail has a horizontal opening through which the staircase can be seen from the ground floor. This isn't just a detail: the opening both accentuates and conceals the staircase in the same way that clothing serves to both accentuate and conceal the body. And in all of Van Duysen's projects, particular care has been given to the ceiling. It is not uncommon, even in well-designed buildings, for the ceilings to be neglected, but – to Van Duysen – each surface of a space is equally important. In the case of his Sportmax flagship store in Milan (p. 64), Van Duysen manages to tie the staircase and ceiling together in a way that is simple yet highly effective. He deliberately chose an open staircase structure, whose horizontal aspect echoes the long, aluminium profiles that house the lighting, which in turn contrast with the strong, horizontal design of the dark display stand. It is these and other design features which give the store its dimension of space and unexpected depth.

In the baroque period, it was popular to divide broad staircases into two symmetrical flights halfway up. One outstanding example of a double staircase can be found at the Alte Pinakothek in Munich. Designed by Hans Doellgast and built in 1950, two identical sets of stairs are set end to end and span a whole floor. Thanks to the photography of Thomas Schütte, this staircase has gained almost iconic status. Van Duysen has incorporated double staircases into many of his projects, including residential and commercial premises. In the Copyright Bookshop (p. 124), housed in the ModeNatie Antwerp, two separate staircases lead to the mezzanine floors. Although hidden behind a wall, it is still

RA Residence, Antwerp, 1998–1999

clear where they are. The same material is used for the first four steps before the staircase splits, leaving customers in no doubt as to which way to go. But Van Duysen has done more here than just fit out a bookstore. Being inside the space is a bit like being inside a church or temple. The double-height nave, two adjoining aisles and additional floor evoke the church of St Carolus Borromeus in Antwerp, an association which has less to do with the decor of this 17th-century building than with the structural composition of the space.

In choosing the materials for the project, Van Duysen was influenced both by the work of Austrian architect Adolf Loos and by the building itself. The mottled Spanish marble, used for the floor, the first four steps of the stairs, the central display area and the counter, creates a distinct ambience. It is the clash between this material and the white plaster which gives the interior its special character. What could be nicer than the texture of hewn marble? It isn't man's creation, but rather Nature herself that is responsible for the wonderful combination of colours and shapes.

At the Brasserie National, also housed in Antwerp's ModeNatie, Van Duysen made the most of the high space to create a traditional and elegant interior. This was also the first outing for the chairs that he designed for B&B Italia. But above all, it was the architect's use of travertine, the material chosen by Mies van der Rohe for the iconic Barcelona Pavilion, which gave Van Duysen's work such an anti-fashion feel. Van Duysen dares to use words such as 'beauty' and 'elegance', concepts which don't feature very often in modern-day architectural criticism.

The main role of the architect, as Loos often said, is to create space. The space remains long after the inhabitants have gone. Then other people take over the interior, with *their* objects and furniture. But surrounding oneself with carefully chosen objects is important to Van Duysen. His own apartment (p. 24), renovated in 1998, is testament to this. He chose to leave the large living room intact, the essence here being the abundance of natural light and number of particular objects, from a lounge chair to a large screw from a wine press. This isn't a design product showroom, it's an intimate space. A place to relax at the end of the day.

A view of the Scheldt

In the 1930s, Le Corbusier produced a city plan for Antwerp. He drew a series of wonderful perspectives, all of which used the great bend in the Scheldt as the structuring element: Antwerp's left bank gripped by the movement of the river. Any architect would recognize this as a prime location, and Van Duysen was no exception, using its visual potential as a point of departure for his penthouse design (p. 206). The first phase of the project consisted of converting the second floor into office space, while the second phase concerned the large extension above the building, a penthouse on three floors. Not only was the view over the river

too good an opportunity to miss, but the wide view to the rear – the city skyline with all its towers – was also impressive. The project was complex from a construction point of view, not least because the standards that had to be met were not normal for this type of housing. In order to reduce the weight of the project as much as possible, Van Duysen opted to use a metal skeleton and wooden floors. Where some of the walls are faced with natural stone, the overall weight was reduced by using an aluminium honeycomb with a natural stone veneer.

As is often the case, it isn't possible to fully comprehend the spatial concept from the floor plans. The cross-section shows a displaced void running through all three levels. This creates fascinating new diagonal perspectives, turning the penthouse into a fluid space, with a direct visual link between the living area and the home gym. Here, too, a straight, continuous staircase links the three floors, running parallel to the front façade, with a landing on the second floor. The intentionally dark walls of this vertical circulation zone increase the pull of the light. In this project, Van Duysen and his colleagues demonstrated complete control at every technical and compositional level. It is a synthesis project, where each detail contributes to the whole.

Urban densification

Antwerp has had a tradition of enclosed courtyards since the baroque period. In most cases, the outdoor spaces around urban blocks were simply filled in with secondary buildings. The S Residential Complex (p. 234) is particularly interesting because it is more than a self-contained building project, it is also an urban-planning operation that seeks to upgrade an enclosed space. Instead of designing the living areas of the apartments so that they face the street, everything is oriented towards a new inner courtyard, where there is a tree and climbing plants. On the Leopoldstraat side, there are shop premises at ground-floor level that lead to a large space at the back, formerly an art auctioneer's premises, which has been integrated into the project. As far as the apartments are concerned, again the architect's aim was to try to achieve as great a sense of depth as possible, although large, folding doors meant that it was still possible to create separate areas. Each living room has vertical windows which can be fully opened.

A project on the Korenlei in Ghent is another case in point where the architect was required to manage an important historical context. The baroque façade had to be preserved, so the only place where alterations could be made was in the roof area. Instead of fitting mundane sloping roof windows, Van Duysen cut into the roof, but sought at the same time to retain a sense of visual unity. The roof was covered with Belgian bluestone and sits harmoniously alongside the windows. The result is a smart view of Ghent's historic towers from the top floor, just as the client requested. The effect of lowering the eaves

and using unusual materials serves to both emphasize the intervention and make it disappear at the same time.

The move to larger projects

In the 1990s, Van Duysen was one of a number of young Belgian architects awarded contracts by the bank and insurance group BAC. His modifications to the branch banks in Kalmthout and Brasschaat show a high degree of sensitivity for materials. In the Kalmthout branch, the location and design of the staircase transform a functional component into a quasi-sculptural object.

The project which first brought Van Duysen to the attention of the architectural world was undoubtedly the Concordia Offices in Waregem (p. 80). Located on an unremarkable industrial estate, this building was an addition to the company's existing complex. The parking spaces are situated at the front of the building, with access to the understated entrance via an interesting route, a path between the fully glazed front and a raised, cobbled area. This raised, linear strip means that while staff in the office can see the road from their desks, they themselves cannot be seen from the road. The floor plan is extremely clear, and the openness sought by the architect does not elude him. The outer shell and interior are punctuated by three double-height sections which flood the building with light. For Van Duysen and client alike, the project was about more than creating space for office furniture. Indeed, the interior developed into a space where art was prominent, a sort of office-museum hybrid. We all know that jobs can disappear, but a building's potential, and power, remains, even as it gracefully takes on a new purpose.

Lately, Van Duysen has been in receipt of larger contracts, a few of which are still in the design phase. In 2004, he took part in a competition to build a new crematorium in Sint-Niklaas, 140 metres long and linear in structure. According to his design, the two main parts of the project – the furnaces and the service block – will be given a completely different expression by means of the materials used. The section housing the furnaces will be made of glass, while the main building will be constructed from natural stone. The proposal pays great attention to incorporating the building into the surrounding landscape. A project for a school building in Kortrijk is likewise still at the competition design stage.

Most of Van Duysen's projects are set in an urban context, and this is certainly true of his proposal for the Ackermans-Van Haaren office. This was located in an area dominated by late-19th-century buildings, and had a pronounced vertical façade. Using this verticality as a starting point, Van Duysen designed a gable with narrow slats to vary the spatial distribution. He used the same solution at the rear of the building, which looks out onto a courtyard. In 2004, Van Duysen won a contract to build a new youth hostel in Antwerp's

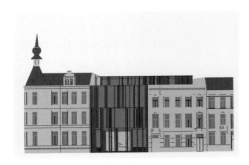

A·VH Offices, Antwerp, 2002

historic city centre. Rather than building across the whole of the available plot, he opted for a more compact design, freeing up space for a public square in front of the hostel. This was particularly good from an urban-planning point of view, given the built-up nature of the immediate surrounding area and the orientation of the plot. The façade has a rigid, vertical pattern, but the windows, simple in form, are nevertheless highly engineered. There is no interplay between horizontal and vertical elements, with Van Duysen coming down firmly on the side of Auguste Perret when the latter argued with Le Corbusier that 'a window, like a man, should stand upright'.

Van Duysen continues to enjoy acclaim outside Belgium. His first overseas contracts were interior design projects in Mallorca (p. 42) and New York (p. 68), but architectural contracts soon followed. His 2005 design for an office building in Beirut uses the layering of the façade as the point of departure for the rest of the concept. Projects in Hamburg, Paris, Milan and Dubai are also ongoing.

Towards 'visually silent' architecture

For Van Duysen, there is no need to clamour for attention with virtuoso shapes. Anyone who studies his smaller work can see that he is not an industrial designer, but rather someone who approaches the world with the tactility of an architect and can shape objects so that they inspire familiarity and trust in spite of any novelty. Common to all Van Duysen's designs is an aversion to ostentation; he has no interest in short-term visual effect. Instead, his works are characterized by their identifiability and recognizability. The products may well be diverse in nature, but the underlying philosophy is always the same, whether it's a chair collection for B&B Italia (p. 130), a chandelier for Swarovski (p. 142), a kitchen for Obumex (p. 180), tableware for When Objects Work (p. 178) or a coat stand for Viccarbe (p. 194). His design for a desk for Bulo (p. 170) is pure architecture: furniture created through the correct juxtaposition of vertical and horizontal surfaces.

Van Duysen's work is a rejection of all that is showy and strives to be spectacular. As a result, he is not one of those architects currently much lauded by the media. His work is not about intellectual posturing or producing superficial ideas. For him, tangibility is all – the transformation of an idea into a real, surprising, visual whole. Tactile enjoyment and visual experience reign supreme. It would be all too easy to describe Van Duysen's work as 'minimalist'; indeed, I have gone out of my way to avoid using that word here. We can be too quick sometimes to categorize people's work. Van Duysen clearly does not take a postmodern approach, combining multiple images to create a certain atmosphere. In fact, his work could even be seen as the antithesis to the current 'deco-design' trend. He chooses another way, and takes ownership of the vocabulary. In a world polluted by visual stimuli, surely architecture has another role.

Youth Hostel, Antwerp, 2004–2010

Brasserie National, Antwerp, 2000–2002

It should not try to emulate ephemera, such as fashion or pop videos. It is destined to fulfil a different function, if only because of the length of the entire architectural process. This problem was clearly expressed by Adolf Loos at the beginning of the 20th century. The job of architecture is to create authentic contexts in which we can find shelter. If an architect opts for simplicity, this does not automatically mean he is trying to handcuff his client. The idea of the architect as some kind of saviour come to show people how they should be living in the modern age is long gone. It is more to do with the search for intense simplicity to counterbalance the visual violence in the world. This quest for noble simplicity has nothing to do with laziness: it is the result of a conviction that human beings need harmonious spaces. It is much more a petition for a return to an approach in which silence can claim its place.

Van Duysen's work is in no way ascetic or dispassionate; it seeks to control the space. The process of simplification is not a form of simplism or indolence. The decision to choose silence is a conscious one, and the power of the atmosphere is a direct result of the materials used and the opportunities offered by the space. If an architect abstains from the over-consumption of fleeting images, his work will reflect this attitude of simplification. This can lead to the paradox that precise and simple execution is frequently more expensive whilst appearing to deliver less. In a world in which we are bombarded with images, many people cannot understand or accept this.

At the beginning of his career, Van Duysen's designs were featured in a number of Belgian lifestyle magazines, leading many to believe, incorrectly, that he was a trendy interior designer. Fortunately his work also appeared in international trade journals around the same time, and readers were able to see that Van Duysen was more interested in structuring spaces than in dressing them. Although their work is different, it is possible to compare Van Duysen to the late Maarten Van Severen and the Belgian partnership of Claire Bataille and Paul Ibens, all of whom have favoured intensity over spectacular images. Perhaps this approach, which is about experiencing concrete enjoyment of one's home, is specifically Belgian. Internationally, Van Duysen's work can be compared to that of David Chipperfield and John Pawson. It is perhaps no coincidence that both these men, now well-known architects, began by designing apartment and store interiors.

> 'Verwechseln Sie bitte nicht das Einfache mit dem Simplen'
> (Don't confuse minimal with simple)
> — Mies van der Rohe

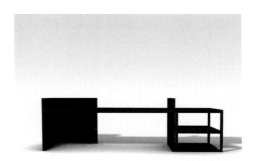

Desk for Bulo, 2004

Projects

1993 to the present

VVD Residence 1

Antwerp, Belgium

1993

This third-floor apartment in a former spice and rubber warehouse became Van Duysen's home when he set up practice in Antwerp after years of working abroad. It has proved to be a fertile environment in which to experiment with his trademark meditative and sensual spaces, and has been the stage for many of his own furniture designs.

The layout of the apartment is slung around an internal light well, with three glazed sides from which to borrow light. Another unusual feature is the long and narrow living room, of which two walls have generous astragal windows overlooking an unexciting urban fabric. The plan, although divided into rooms, retains a certain flow, as most of the spaces have internal glazed screens and uninterrupted views into the adjacent rooms. A smaller light well at the back of the flat provides yet more fresh air and light.

Van Duysen has left the original elements untouched, and has simply sought to enhance them by screening unwanted views and retaining privacy. The existing wooden floors were sanded and left unfinished, the tiled floors restored, and the walls decorated with a warm and minimal palette. The carefully selected rugs, textiles, *objets trouvés* and pieces of furniture complete a look of sophisticated simplicity, and create a language that is entirely Van Duysen's own. Over the years, this language has become more refined, perhaps – the furniture becoming more taut and more geometric – but has always stayed true to the essential qualities of a home for living in: warmth, light and well-being.

AK Residence

Antwerp, Belgium

1994

In order to make the most of the generous existing space, this 1950s luxury flat in the centre of Antwerp was stripped of all interior decoration and a new layout skilfully designed, all with the intention of freeing the occupant from the constraints of the traditional apartment. A long corridor extends from one end of the flat to the other, passing through interconnected zones. The furnishings form an integral part of the architecture, and wardrobes and closets are concealed behind sliding doors without visible tracks or hinges. The doors, too, are invisible, built into the walls in a pattern of interlocking panels that freely offer visual communication between the spaces.

Japanese influences and an ascetic spirit are present here; flow and continuity are enhanced by a conscious limiting of materials, details and spatial changes, creating a serene atmosphere. The building materials used contribute to the mood of the space. The play of light and shade against the soft off-white, plastered walls, unsullied by base boards or mouldings, the wide-planked oak floors, the Moroccan tiles that surround a glass mosaic bathtub, and the large oak wall panels are all juxtaposed with the cold, shiny metal of the industrial kitchen. The balance of the warmth of the materials with the rigour of the plan provides an intuitive sense of harmony unusual in an urban setting.

AK Residence

A Silent Sophistication

I love Vincent's work. It leaves one off-centred. It's unusual and has a sense of composition – far from coldness, excess, fashions and trends, and with a sense of tradition applied to modernity that I have only found in Japan. His is an art of matter, a material presence. A perceivable genius loci of diffused serenity.

I love Vincent's contradictions – positive and successful contradictions – as a designer, architect and person. His qualities as an individual permeate his design and live in his architecture. Elegance, equilibrium and contemporaneity emerge from a volcanic, eruptive and energetic personality. This mix of purity and energy forms an organic vision of space that respects the relationship between elements and architecture, a silent sophistication that doesn't need to show off – far from minimalist definitions, far from entertainment architecture, far from memory, sterility. A deceptive perception.

A still photograph cannot give a full sense of Vincent's spaces, which are only wholly appreciable through personal experience, with mutating light conditions. The refined use of light, shadow and filters are active elements of his projects. I love Vincent's connections. He is a true architect and a true designer, rather than an architect who designs or a designer who works with space. Like Maddalena De Padova, Vincent has that rare talent to create a dialogue between elements, a natural conversation between objects, furniture, materials and light; a wooden floor takes on the same dignity of a work of art, a sofa, a beam of light. This tactile, visual and sensual communication is a direct correlation that De Padova learned in her relationship with Charles and Ray Eames, that gives a sense of real connection through things. Another association that comes to mind is the Japanese architect, Kengo Kuma, whose Lotus House combines natural elegance with materiality. I like Vincent's interest in the art world and photography, his pragmatism, his burning personality. A perfectionist in a natural way.

An electrified tabula rasa. A soul in flame. An attention on surface and the skin of things. A capacity for adaptive reuse. An atemporal vision. An Eleusinian mystery.

Patricia Urquiola

Designs for Life

Vincent Van Duysen is often included in lists of 'minimalist architects', yet he has never considered himself a minimalist, nor does he welcome the label. It could be said, however, that his architecture is certainly based on the stripping away of elements. So what is it that sets it apart from minimalism?

In Van Duysen's early interior designs, his language had not yet been clearly defined. But if we think of the minimalism featured in Herbert Ypma's *London Minimum* (1996), for example, clear differences were already emerging. While minimalism is almost an abstraction, the essential nature of Van Duysen's projects lets the materiality of the spaces breathe, allowing the perception of the volumes and colours that replace ornament. The materials, commonly used but reinterpreted in a new way, are stripped of any kind of artifice and are reborn in surfaces that are contemporary in texture and appearance, yet are immersed in their own kind of tradition.

Van Duysen's interiors extend naturally into his furniture, which in turn grows out of industrial production methods. These are not industrial designs, but pieces made to fit into designed environments, thus creating a sense of unity: niches that curve around sofas and beds, along with upholstered seats or comfortable armchairs. Bathroom or kitchen storage solutions hide everything from view, with a rigour that leaves no room for hesitation. This rigour is partly inspired by the grand purists of the past, but is also highly contemporary, particularly in the purity of the pieces created through the use of new technology.

His industrial design projects are something else again. Even in their names, his works reveal a desire to create repeatable archetypes. Although intended for mass production, his designs seem to be a series of unique pieces: 'Chair', 'Table'.

And here we go back to the completeness of his architecture, to his designs for spaces. A spatial continuum in which interior design and furniture are integrated, creating an experience that can be interpreted afresh every day. An element so modest and yet so present requires someone with an equally strong personality to live with it.

Roberta Mutti

On Beauty

> The Westerner uses silver and steel and nickel tableware, and polishes it to a fine brilliance, but we object to that practice. While we do sometimes indeed use silver for tea kettles, decanters or sake cups, we prefer not to polish it. On the contrary, we begin to enjoy it only when the lustre has worn off, when it has begun to take on a dark, smoky patina. Almost every householder has had to scold an insensitive maid who has polished away the tarnish so patiently waited for.
>
> Junichiro Tanizaki, *In Praise of Shadows*

Some things tend to fascinate us at first glance. Sometimes the fascination lasts throughout that first encounter. Sometimes it lasts through countless encounters from then on. So, do we love things that last, or do the things we love end up lasting? Either way, time can be taken as a measure, to determine the empathy level between us and what is around us.

Beauty is not transitory. It does not belong to any time, but remains beyond time. Beauty is such a still thing that requires stillness to be recognized. It is useless to search for it. The beauty in Vincent Van Duysen's works is the natural outcome of a conceptual process, which focuses on achieving maximum depuration without any sort of design trickery. Authenticity, we might call it. After all, we don't always have to wait for time to pass to know that something will last.

Manuel and Francisco Aires Mateus,
with Valentino Capelo de Sousa

Poetic Sensualism

The work of Vincent is all about sensuality and sensitivity. It reflects his ability to translate his strong connection to his clients and to the objects he is designing into poetic expressions that transcend the physical.

It is a genuine drive to create an elevating experience for people, beyond stylistic concerns, that brings us together.

Vladimir Djurovic

Natan Shop

Brussels, Belgium

1995–1996

One of the many projects Van Duysen has undertaken for Natan, a well-known Belgian fashion house, the design for this shop in Brussels takes its cue from the pure, essential lines of the space and furnishings. Light becomes a fundamental factor in the perception of the geometry of the building.

Laid out over two levels, the design plays with the vertical dilatation of the architectural volume, and creates visual openings that allow one's gaze to run freely over the contours of the interior. Natural light from the large windows on the upper floor invades and saturates the stark, white walls and partitions of the floor below. The staircase is enhanced and transformed from a mere functional element into a forceful architectonic presence, in contrast to the rarefied emptiness of the spaces.

The furnishings are also reduced to an essential minimum, and are perfectly integrated with the neutrality of the space and of the garments themselves, which are hung from minimal hooks like artworks in a gallery.

Natan Shop

DB·VD Residence

Sint-Amandsberg, Belgium

1994–1997

This ultra-simplified, monolithic brick building occupying a plot on a typical Flemish lot development was created by reinterpreting the rules governing sloping roofs and cornice height.

Apertures in the side walls reinforce the central circulation zone; the bricks used for the front façade are also employed here at equal intervals. A series of sliding doors on the ground floor enable the communal area to be closed off for privacy, and opened up for continuity.

Whereas the purpose of the circulation zone on the ground floor is to link one space to another, on the first floor its job is to act as a buffer between the master bedroom and the other bedrooms. This separation of the upstairs rooms is reinforced by the introduction of the exterior materials into the interior, and by the retraction of the glass façade behind the outer brick wall.

M Residence

Mallorca, Spain

1996–1997

The intention of the renovation of an old rural house set inland on the island of Mallorca, with its impressive portico and two adjacent buildings that now function as an office for the owner and lodgings for the caretakers, was to preserve the spirit of the original Spanish *finca*. Inside, the spaces are clean, essential, just like the furnishing elements used throughout the building.

The resulting atmosphere is one of absolute balance, permeated by a feeling of leisure and relaxation. The traditional Mallorcan flooring of pebblestone embedded in cement has been used both inside and out, creating a seamless continuity between the house and landscape. Only the house's exterior defines a true physical and visual barrier, accentuating the sensation of privacy. This sensation does not change upon entering the house: the entrance area is a large, empty room, enhanced by wood panelling that conceals the entrance to the guest bathroom. The only decorative presence in this space is a washstand, carved from a single block of stone and inserted into a niche.

The rigorous character of the furnishing solutions – simple planes, elementary volumes – is accentuated by such rich materials as sanded and stained oak, stone, marble and ceramics. Porcelain light fixtures by Belgian designer Jos Devriendt also add to the overall feeling of luxurious simplicity.

M Residence

VH Residence

Lokeren, Belgium

1995–1998

Behind the unchanged 1930s façade, this house, which had been built as one of a series of five dwellings all designed by the same architect, has been dismantled and completely restyled. The goal of such a radical transformation was to introduce light and space into a very narrow structure.

There were two major considerations with regard to the project. The first of these was the construction of spaces along a horizontal axis, stretching all the way from the entrance of the house to the bottom of the garden. The opening along this axis makes it possible to fully experience the depth of the building, while the position of the staircase against the partition wall makes maximum use of the available space. The second was ensuring that the three-storey-high central atrium, topped by a cupola and adjacent to the living area on the first floor, acts as a luminous hinge for the surrounding rooms. By opening up the back frontage completely, the living area has been remarkably extended. This transparency creates a more effective relationship between the different spaces and their functions.

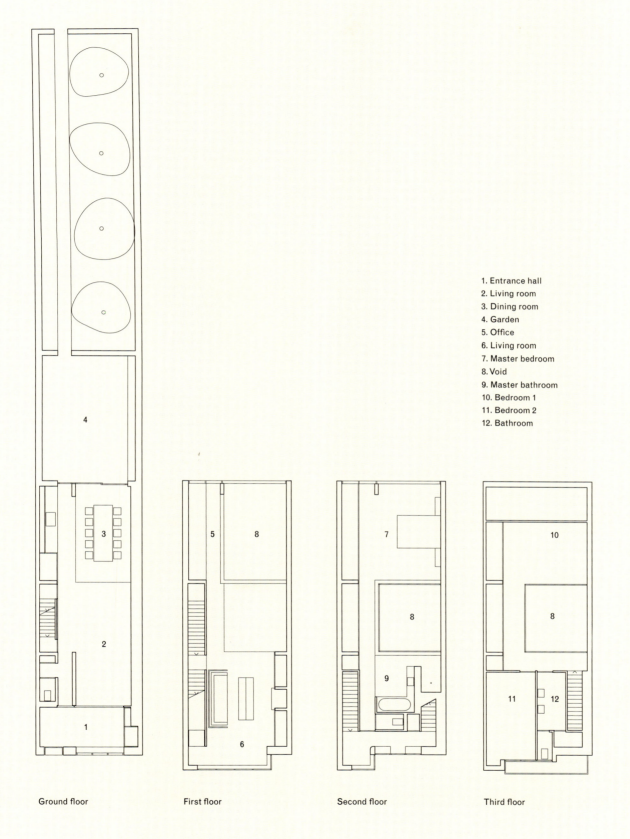

1. Entrance hall
2. Living room
3. Dining room
4. Garden
5. Office
6. Living room
7. Master bedroom
8. Void
9. Master bathroom
10. Bedroom 1
11. Bedroom 2
12. Bathroom

Ground floor   First floor   Second floor   Third floor

0 ⊢⊢⊢⊢⊢⊣ 5m

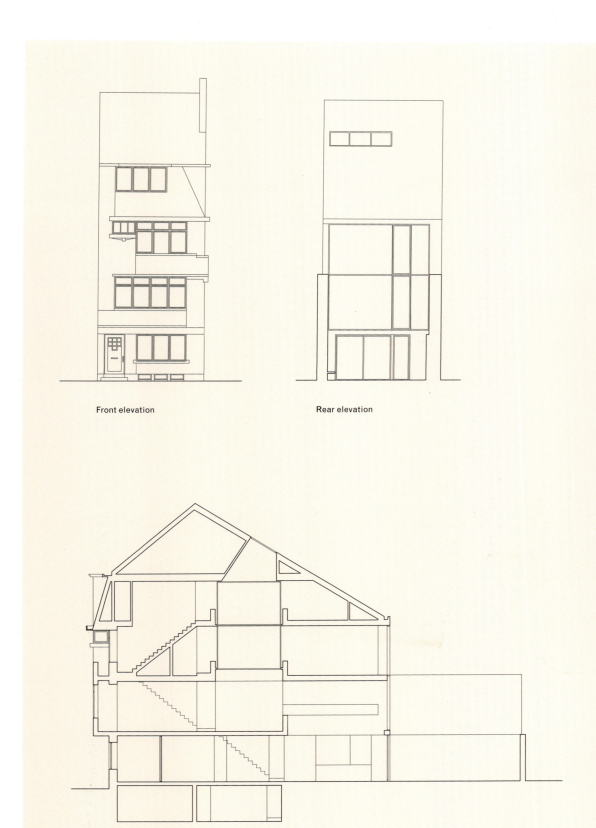

Front elevation

Rear elevation

Section

VH Residence

V Residence

Brussels, Belgium

1997–1998

This traditional townhouse in the centre of Brussels, bought by an art lover with a considerable collection of contemporary art, had undergone a crude renovation in the 1970s, and consequently not much remained of the original character and atmosphere of the building. The brief was simple: to provide a home for both client and collection, and thus create a neutral, almost gallery-like, setting.

Only two items were retained and carefully restored: the original 19th-century winding staircase and the street elevation. The generous staircase forms the focal point of the entrance hall, with natural light filtering down from a skylight through a translucent screen. This arrangement serves to give the light an ethereal quality, while revealing nothing of the banal structure behind it.

Although the refurbishment was extensive and many of the walls relined to provide simple, clean backgrounds, the original bourgeois layout, complete with servants' quarters and basement kitchen, has been respected. The kitchen, which serves all levels via a service lift and staircase, has merely been updated with an architectural cooking element in natural stone. This space is naturally and symmetrically lit via two *cours anglaises* that sit below garden level.

The classical character of the house has also been preserved on the other levels, providing the sense of calm required to effectively display works of art, while the limited palette of materials and minimal detailing sustain flow throughout the building. The rear elevation has not been completely opened up and glazed, as is often the case with existing townhouses, and the width of the narrow windows have been left untouched. The resulting elevation has a strong, monolithic and timeless presence, enhanced by the deep reveals of the windows and the effect of light and shade. Its verticality is reflected internally by the insertion of very tall, dark-stained doors wherever possible.

The floor area of the formal dining room on the upper level has been pulled back from the garden elevation and is connected to the living area below via a void that extends the width of the house.

Less Is More? More With Less, More With Light!

I only ever write about architects whose work interests me and seems worthwhile. The architecture of Vincent Van Duysen is certainly worthwhile. Although he is still very young (forty-five being young for an architect), his built works have what I see as the essential quality of 'lasting through time'. Although they are highly contemporary, they are not informed by the capricious styles that now fill many glossy publications and make them appear more like fashion magazines. His works are both rigorous and logical, and also very beautiful.

A Rejection of Minimalism
First of all, I must state that in my opinion, and perhaps in that of Van Duysen himself, despite the fact that he is often included in lists of minimalist architects, his architecture is not minimalist but something different, something much deeper. Converting the 'less is more' approach into what I have often described as a 'more with less' strategy is something very distinct from minimalism proper.

To my mind, minimalists are those who don't know what to say and so say nothing. And with their mute mystery and their harsh, frozen spaces, they try to make us believe that something is interesting. It's like bad poetry. But nothing could be further from reality. Good poetry, true poetry, is far from 'literary minimalism'; it is the fascinating ability to choose just a few precise words that can take us to a place of sublime beauty, deeply moving our hearts and minds – like Shakespeare or St John of the Cross. 'More with less' architecture works in the same way. No more and no less, just enough. Will the so-called critics ever understand this? Van Duysen is no more and no less than a poet of contemporary architecture, and a good one.

Close to the Sky: Private Residence, Antwerp
High up like the head of a building, this penthouse and office overlooking the Scheldt seem to be a clear expression, in the face of traditional architecture which requires sloping planes to get rid of rain and snow through the force of gravity, that modern architecture proposes a more rational solution. New architecture gives us the gift of being able to build a penthouse like a magical place, open to the sky and the sun, giving a privileged view of the landscape – a lesson learned from Le Corbusier.

Van Duysen and many other contemporary architects work with different elements. Steel, large planes of transparent glass, and synthetic weatherproofing solutions have not only freed roof spaces from the ground, but have also made it possible to create profound works from spaces open to the sky. New architecture, the kind that embodies the *esprit nouveau* of Le Corbusier, too often remains unbuilt. When I stand on my roof terrace in Madrid, high up in the sky, and can see the many recent plans that remain unrealized, I am constantly surprised.

The spaces that Van Duysen has created at the top of his buildings are particularly interesting. They are like manifestos of the most glorious radicalism and transparency.

Like Giraffes: Concordia Offices
If we stand in front of the magnificent Concordia Offices in Waregem, which look as if they have just been built, we can imagine that the orderly row of tall blocks are in fact giraffes, raising their necks to reach the light in a well-ordered and carefully calculated rhythm. For an architect, rhythm as a means of controlling dimensions and proportions, what was once called eurythmy, remains an important goal, one that Van Duysen seems to be pursuing and achieving. The tall blocks of the Concordia building serve to both take in light and create dilations within the interior space. An indivisible conjunction of light and space: pure architecture.

A Piece of Heaven: Crematorium, Sint-Niklaas
What is there to be said about the shining piece of heaven that is the crematorium at Sint-Niklaas? The translucent box, solid and powerful, seems from the outside to be a white cloud, geometricized into a white parallelepiped. A white cloud descended to earth, from which might emerge at any moment the smiling figure of St Nicholas, pleased to inhabit such a glorious abode.

The beautiful interior shows a classical division between the stereotomic and the tectonic, the clear division suggested by Gottfried Semper and cited by Kenneth Frampton, which so many of us have used as a teaching device in our classes and in our architecture. The lower part, linked to the ground, is material, as if excavated: stereotomic, offering rest to mankind. The upper part, linked to the sky, is luminous and ethereal, full of light and air: tectonic, offering satisfaction to the soul. Or as the master would have said, 'satisfaction of the spirit'. A divine box, clear and bright, that deserves to have been built.

And All Things Van Duysen
We could continue to analyze Van Duysen's work and the conclusion would be the same. From Block 20-02 in Beirut to the beautiful Copyright Bookshop in Antwerp's fashion museum, from the amazing loft in New York to the fascinating VVD Residence in Antwerp – all of Van Duysen's work is of exceptional quality.

An architect who is clear and straightforward, logical and intelligent, one who recalls the words of Konstantin Melnikov when Melnikov described his own house in Moscow: 'Being able to do whatever I wanted, I asked Architecture to let me strip her of her marble gown, to wash off her make-up and show herself as she truly is, naked as a goddess, young and graceful. And as befits a true beauty, she refused to be cheerful and complacent.'

Vincent Van Duysen, a true architect.

Alberto Campo Baeza

Sportmax Shop
Milan, Italy

1999

The building has been stripped back to expose its basic structure. For the interior, the palette of materials was also reduced to its absolute minimum: concrete tile floors, brickwork walls with a thin, mortar-based finish, and pieces of furniture made from aluminium and wood, together with custom-made light beams on the ceiling.

The roughness of the materials used is in sharp contrast with the refinement of the clothing; both contribute to an atmosphere of purified space. The free-standing furniture further intensifies the sensation of purity. Aluminium containers function as display cases and offer a wide variety of possibilities for displaying the clothes without interfering with the typology of the space.

SPORTMAX

66

Sportmax Shop

RH-BH Residence
New York, USA

1999

The neighbourhood of SoHo is well known for its 19th-century industrial loft apartments, and the client, a young Flemish entrepreneur, wished to refurbish his own loft, with its fantastic views overlooking the Manhattan skyline.

The essentially male atmosphere of the city has been translated internally through the use of strong colours, a New York palette of dark wood and leather against a background of white and red, and a rigorous layout with day and night zones, delineated by the custom-made, oversized furniture. The night zone has been divided into dedicated rooms and annexes, leaving a large, open-plan living area for entertaining, which features a dining table with ample space for sixteen people and high-backed benches that screen the window. Both the original cast-iron pillars and visible air-conditioning system have been completely painted out in black.

The seating area has been separated off with a long, low storage bench, clad in suede. The traditional focal point of the living room – the fireplace – has been replaced by the more modern television, hidden behind a sliding screen. White walls, black-stained oak parquet flooring and large, white-painted window frames give this space a strong identity. From the living area, a corridor leads to the bedrooms. The master bedroom is almost Spartan in its layout and colours in contrast to the guest rooms, which are painted in rich red and furnished with contrasting black-and-white furniture.

The apartment is characterized by a conscious spareness, with the furnishings used as essential elements within the space. The strong colours and contrasts, together with the pure geometric forms, create a setting worthy of a 1940s American crime novel, updated for the 21st century.

RH-BH Residence

RH-BH Residence

Wash Basin

for Obumex

1999

This simple, minimal design for Obumex is the embodiment of Van Duysen's architecture in miniature. Orthogonal geometry reigns supreme in the definition of the volumes; the resulting objects conceal their function – revealed only by the tall faucet – while flaunting the geometric purity of their forms. The washstands are in wood with steel basins, from which the tap emerges, mixer control to one side.
It is impossible to contaminate the nearby space with the usual accoutrements and accessories. The fronts of the units remain elegantly pristine as the washstands contain integrated storage, accessible through a slit on the side.

Fashion Club

Antwerp, Belgium

1998–1999

This venue contains a number of different activities on different levels, with showrooms, retail outlets, service spaces on the first two floors, and offices and a restaurant on the third. Located in a 19th-century building (as is evident from the cast-iron structure with its neoclassical columns and thick beams), the clean, clear rigour of the plan and the original architectural elements dictate the decoration and compositional rhythm.

No divider systems have been used to preserve the horizontal continuity of the space, which has been accentuated by the presence of elementary, geometric furnishings that perform the roles of both functional objects and a kind of domestic architecture within the architecture. Long oak tables and stools in almost monastic shapes, and interiors based on the perfect orthogonal design of intersecting planes, create volumes of disarming simplicity. The layout is extremely flexible, allowing the space to adapt to the various requirements.

The sensation of tranquillity is underlined by the light that filters through the large, acrylic panels, creating an atmosphere that invites visitors to relax and enjoy small, everyday pleasures – from a cup of coffee to lunch with friends – far from the frenzied pace of one of the busiest port cities in northern Europe.

Fashion Club

Concordia Offices

Waregem, Belgium

1998–2000

The modular design for this new office complex, created for a Belgian textile firm, incorporated three oversized light boxes to reflect the company's industrial connections. The main entrance is located beneath the first of these light boxes; once inside, the axis of the long catwalk leading from the parking area is repeated in the central circulation.

The light boxes both anchor the site into the landscape and create a strong spatial effect in the interior, enhanced by plenty of natural light. A sober façade of concrete and glass panels encloses the old, existing building; this use of a limited selection of specific materials defines the new structure as a neutral, monolithic form.

Concordia Offices

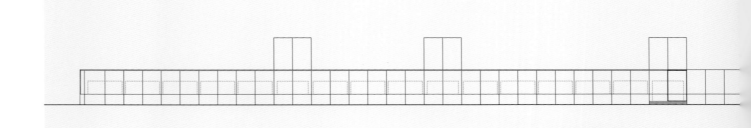

Front elevation

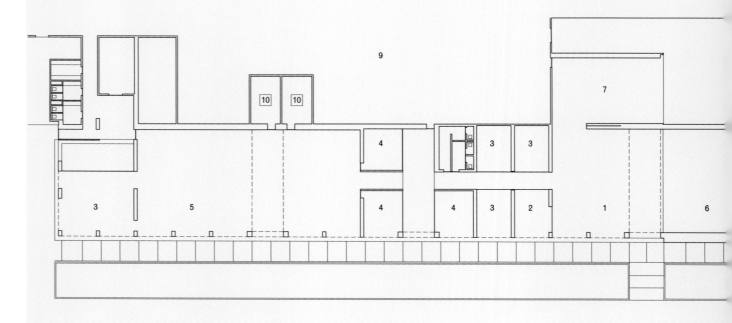

Ground floor

1. Entrance
2. Reception
3. Meeting room
4. Executive office
5. Landscape office
6. Multifunctional room
7. Presentation room
8. Inner courtyard
9. Existing building
10. Existing office
11. Parking

Concordia Offices

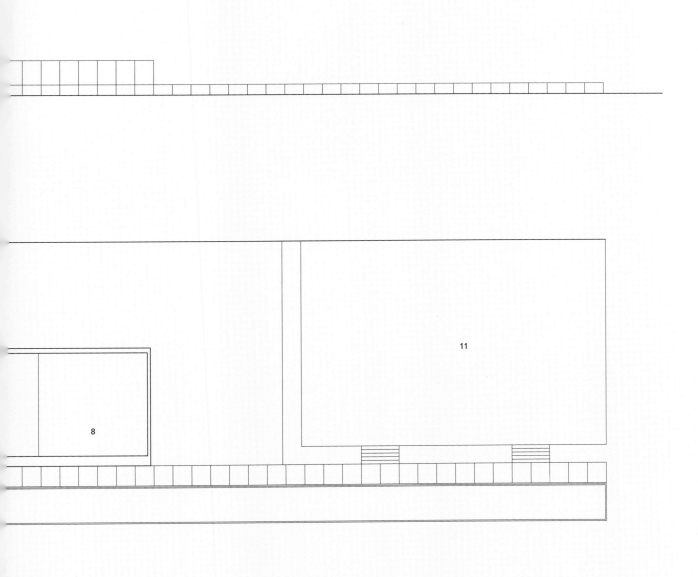

86

Concordia Offices

VL Residence

Bruges, Belgium

1999–2000

In the heart of an ancient and picturesque town, sometimes known as 'Venice of the North' due to its many canals, two adjacent historic townhouses have been transformed into a single family home.

The original character of the buildings, along with the traditional floor plan, have been retained, but a fresh and modern feel has been added through the mix of monumental furniture elements, including an enormous bathtub made out of Carrara marble, which sits under a simple pendant lamp design by the architect, and soothing decorative features like the grey-painted walls and pale oak floorboards. Throughout the house is evidence of the extensive use of reclaimed materials, from the winding staircase and washbasin to the bathtub and flooring.

DC Residence

Waasmunster, Belgium

1998–2001

This site of this project is located in a leafy residential area, and during the summer months is the perfect setting for such outdoor activities as walking, biking or horseback riding. The design of the house, therefore, needs to enable the owners to lead their lives both indoors and out, shielded from the gaze of the many passers-by.

A natural stone wall surrounds the house and serves as a buffer between the public and private zones. It is folded like a limestone envelope around an almost completely transparent ground floor, where the living areas are concentrated. The wall transforms into the patio surface and extends into the interior, taking in such free-standing objects as the washbasin, the kitchen units and the bathroom facilities. To maximize the natural light on the ground floor, only a few walls divide the interior into functional zones. Large, sliding walls and pivoting doors redefine or separate the different spaces. The first floor houses the sleeping areas; the core of this floor is formed by a hidden patio that provides light and views throughout the different rooms and hallways.

Although the architecture is rigorous, the combination of materials and colours make for a soft and inviting home. The warm quality of the stone is underscored by the natural oak finish of the tables and cupboards, and the soft tones of the plastered walls and custom-made furniture enhances the quiet, soothing atmosphere.

DC Residence

DC Residence

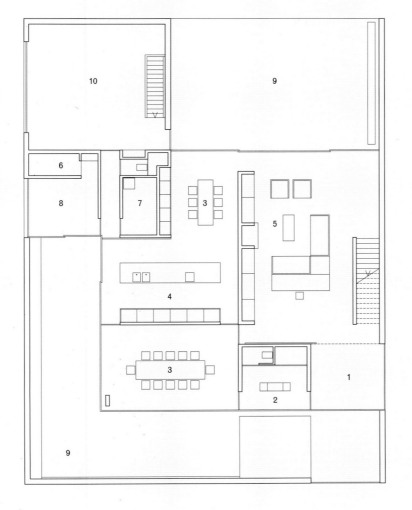

Ground floor

1. Entrance hall
2. Cloakroom
3. Dining room
4. Kitchen
5. Living room
6. Sauna
7. Storage
8. Fitness
9. Terrace
10. Garage

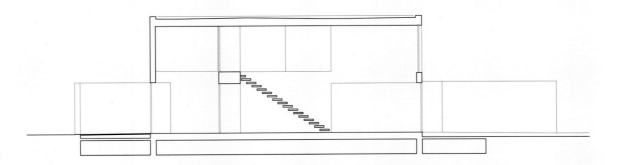

Section

0 |___|___|___|___|___| 5m

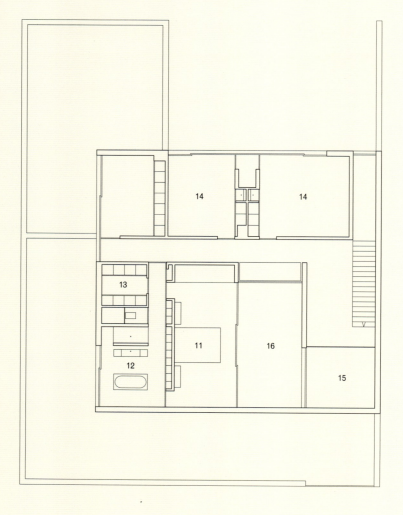

First floor

11. Master bedroom
12. Master bathroom
13. Dressing room
14. Bedroom
15. Void
16. Patio

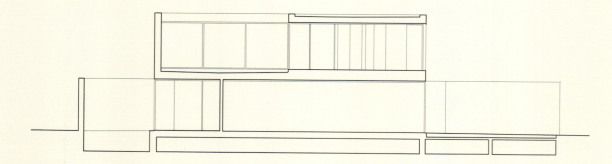

Section

DC Residence

M·VS Residence

Brussels, Belgium

1999–2001

This two-storey penthouse, located in a building designed by Belgian architect Marc Corbiau, is divided into two areas. The large main floor above and smaller guest floor below are organized around a central core, with an open floor plan of shifting volumes.

The main floor was cleared of as many divisions as possible, with only a few interconnected zones that can be hidden away via sliding doors, allowing for a variety of configurations and views through the living spaces. Storage is concealed behind the sliding doors, to both keep the rooms pure and to avoid distracting from the white Carrara marble that has been used throughout for the floors and wall cladding. This unrelenting whiteness provides a striking contrast to the dark oak wall panelling and furniture and the landscape outside, visible between the white volumes. The kitchen, although designed as a very functional space, has the beauty of an abstract marble sculpture, while in the bathroom, the only features are a massive marble bath and long, stretched washbasin in the same material.

This pattern of dark and white is only broken by the client's colourful art collection. It was his express wish to avoid creating a gallery-like setting for his works of art, but to live with them as part of the everyday life of the flat. The neutral colour palette of the interior forms the perfect backdrop.

110

M-VS Residence

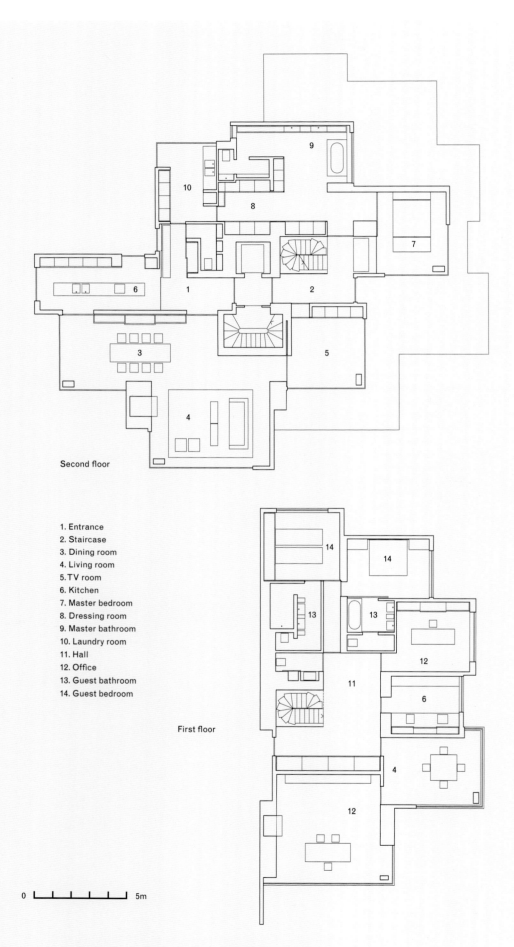

Second floor

1. Entrance
2. Staircase
3. Dining room
4. Living room
5. TV room
6. Kitchen
7. Master bedroom
8. Dressing room
9. Master bathroom
10. Laundry room
11. Hall
12. Office
13. Guest bathroom
14. Guest bedroom

First floor

M-VS Residence

M-VS Residence

Maximalist Austerity

The first interview I did with Vincent – years ago – was about books. It was an enjoyable conversation, and it has stayed with me. As a journalist, one rarely gets the opportunity to talk about anything other than architecture when meeting an architect for the first time. But with Vincent, I couldn't have asked for more: we dove straight into a subject dear to both our hearts and about which we could talk about as equals, as book fans together, without the usual barrier between expert and layman. Now I am convinced that this is the perfect way to start a conversation with an architect.

I still remember how he told me he found books calming, and that he kept part of his book collection in his bedroom. Other people may have found this insignificant, but for me it was highly relevant. I liked the idea, too. At the time there was a lot of fuss being made about minimalism, and Vincent was shoved into this category. But having spoken with him I realized this was nonsense. How can someone who likes to wake up surrounded by books be a minimalist? Since then, I have paid a lot more attention to his work. Not only to the furniture and interiors which appear so often in magazines, but also to the buildings, which attract attention in their 'real' environments: the Concordia Offices in Waregem, for example, or the Antwerp penthouse with its expansive, panoramic view of the Scheldt.

My most recent interview with Vincent took place in his beautifully renovated Flemish townhouse, dating from 1870. And yes, we talked about books. Prompted by the presence of his dachshund George, he showed me a book by the photographer David Douglas Duncan, which contains pictures of Picasso with his dachshund, Lump (*Lump: The Dog Who Ate a Picasso*). This time, however, we also spent time talking about his profession, in particular about his house and current projects, which range from a door handle to an office tower in Beirut.

Nowadays there seem to be quite a few architects who feel the urge to resist fixed geometry. They appear to think that a building can only be interesting if it is shaped like a nest, an egg or a womb. Or they want to cover every surface with lavish designs of flowers, seaweed or climbing plants. They call it *joie de vivre*. Now, I have nothing against joie de vivre, but is it really necessary to claim that straight lines are depressing? What nonsense!

Vincent doesn't use organic lines. His style isn't inspired by nature, nor is he into origami or trendy explosions of colour. Yet one would need to be completely insensitive not to notice that the spaces he designs have an impact. A room or a building can still appeal to the senses without slanting walls or flowers.

Vincent began his career as an interior designer before moving on to building design. Unusual though this path may be, it is nevertheless an advisable one. Designers usually feel a more personal and emotional connection to their interiors than they do to their buildings. In order to be able to design a good interior, one has to have a complete understanding of how people live in their houses, what they think when they wake up, what they do as soon as they get out of bed. This requires an understanding of human nature and the ability to put oneself in someone else's shoes. An architect who has learnt to ask himself whether or not people will feel comfortable in a particular space may perhaps be more likely to appreciate that joie de vivre is dependent on many things, but is not dependent on trendy nature symbolism.

Vincent has a flair for harmony, materials, textures, colours, warmth and detail, and an understanding that is second to none of how to deliberately showcase some elements and conceal others. His approach can be described as simple, calm, harmonious, serene, lucid and sensual, not to mention luxurious, tasteful and extremely attentive to detail. He combines austerity with aestheticism, and brings both to bear in even measure. He has a preference for good-quality, natural materials – ones that are honest, a bit rough round the edges, untreated if possible, and highly tactile. He is not averse to the aesthetic and the poetic, and is interested in sustainability and continuity. With a nod to the past, his work is often traditional, but with a twist. He thinks about the relevance of archetypes today. He is honest in his search and does not choose the easy path. He aims to achieve more than the simple yet ephemeral shock-effect of trendy 'spectacle architecture'. I expect Vincent Van Duysen's work to carry on being appreciated for many years to come.

Chris Meplon

Presence in Space

Buildings are seen, but space is navigated and felt. To perceive space is to sense the void as well as the solid, the materiality of light, and the fluidity of volume. What allows certain environments to create a sense of place, and then to trigger a memory? An elastic play of elements – seen and unseen, spontaneous and formal, intuitive and technical, natural and synthetic – formulate a graphically condensed sensory wonderland.

    The work of Vincent Van Duysen distils perception within a gestural vocabulary of light, movement and surface. Disarmingly simple at first glance, these projects possess a rigorous composition of layered depth, with a vein of stealthy playfulness lurking just beneath the surface. They are highly edited, yet full of presence. The luxury of open space and visual simplicity arrives through the hidden complexity of meticulous planning and programming.

    The body in space implies a dynamic series of relationships. Functional, visual, emotional and kinesthetic experiences overlay desire to communicate a sense of pleasure. Van Duysen anticipates and choreographs this interplay of space and mind, body and perception to reflect a client's needs and desires, thereby translating these desires qualitatively into responsive, sculptural and expressive backdrops for everyday living.

Michael Gabellini

On Vincent

Vincent's work is human;
it possesses many qualities
that we value in people.
It is calm yet determined.
It is reliable yet surprising.
It is sensual, but discreetly so.
It is sober yet spirited.
In other words, it is like a good friend,
like Vincent himself.

Ann Demeulemeester and Patrick Robyn

Capco Offices

Antwerp, Belgium / New York, USA

1999–2001

The starting point for this project was a typical office floor that housed, for the most part, banal corporate spaces without any qualities or expression. Any new scheme would have to be applicable to different building types and locations around the world. The idea was to break with the usual sterile office environment, and create a more domestic space that referenced the prestigious offices of the mid-1930s with their grand ambience. The complete interior was designed in the style of the 1920s and '30s, making use of such materials as ebony, black leather, silver-nickel ironwork and black-tinted glass.

Capco Offices

Copyright Bookshop
Antwerp, Belgium

2000–2001

Having moved from a small space in a narrow alley to the new ModeNatie building, home of Antwerp's fashion museum, this art and architecture bookstore was conceived as a reinterpretation of a traditional library, in conformity with the historic character of the building. The space has been divided into a high central section, flanked on both sides by balconies that are detached from the façade on the street side. At the back of the space, the two balconies end in massive walls, behind which are two identical staircases.

    This spatial set up, in combination with the blank-finished central columns and beam structure, is a striking arrangement of horizontal and vertical lines. Because of this, customers continually experience new views at each point in the shop. In contrast with this clarity, the spaces above and below the balconies were conceived as large-scale niches, into which bookcases could be set. Both the partitions with their book tablets and the ceilings have been carried out in dark wood panelling, and look like boxes slid within the tight, white structure.

The wood panelling evokes a warm and cosy atmosphere, while the simple and sober detailing of furniture and lighting suggest a more contemporary feel. The same can be said of the floor, in dramatically flamed, dark-brown marble, which is consciously reminiscent of the classic Modernist architecture of Mies van der Rohe and Adolf Loos.

The monumental console, desk and central staircase, all in marble, ensure a harmonious balance between old and new. Without the addition of any ornament, the subtle interplay of structure and furniture, including display cases and reading lamps, imbue this modern bookstore with the air of an old-fashioned library.

VVD Collection
for B&B Italia

2002

The design for this collection is not a drastic reinvention, but rather one that has its roots in the design classics of Mies van der Rohe, among others, as well as its own clear identity. The chair has a flat, thin seat atop a slim, steel structure, and its light, floating appearance is emphasized by the addition of one pure curve. By gradually thinning the back of the chair and oversizing the width of the seat, the addition of armrests becomes unnecessary; certain models have an extra cushion for lower back support. The simplicity of the silhouette and the variety of materials make the design extremely flexible.

    The use of muted colours, in combination with the black base and leather finish, allow the day bed to blend in with classic interiors, while the choice of the yellow woollen fabric might appeal to a younger client. The day bed and its derivatives can be placed in different combinations, allowing for sitting, lying down, and all positions in between.

DR Residence

Boechout, Belgium

1999–2002

In undertaking this conversion of a farmhouse and barn, it was soon made clear that the character of the exterior had to be preserved due to planning regulations. The barn was converted into a kitchen and living room, which opened up onto the garden, together with a master bedroom under the pitched roof, while the family room and other bedrooms were housed in the old farmhouse. The lanterns and wooden shutters are new designs by Van Duysen, but evoke traditional forms. Materials that were used outside – Belgian bluestone flooring, grey-tinted pinewood panelling – were repeated in the interior, and a restrained colour palette can be seen throughout, as evidenced by the traditional hand-painted walls.

134

DR Residence

Brasserie National

Antwerp, Belgium

2000–2002

The design brief for the renovation and decoration of the Brasserie National, located in the ModeNatie building, was to create a contemporary restaurant, while respecting the neoclassical character of the existing building. The result is a sober but rich interior, elaborated with contemporary shapes and modern materials. The arrangement of the fixed furniture provides the necessary sophisticated cosiness, while the black-brown ceiling is reminiscent of the smoke-covered ceilings of old, and creates, together with the dark walls, an intimate atmosphere at the bar.

All of the traditional brasserie archetypes have been used and reinterpreted: a waiter station with a copper reading lamp; mirrors and illuminated glazed shelves behind the bar; copper-bronze nameplates and menu trays. Although the materials have been used in a modern way, they are in complete harmony with the decoration as with the character of the building; chairs upholstered in brown leather recall the past glory of Modernist furniture. The arrangement of the interior provides contrasting volumes, in combination with the materials and interior elements, and the interaction between the vertical pillars and the horizontal furniture subtly supports the functional division and circuit. For the seating, prototypes of the VVD Collection for B&B Italia (see p. 130) were used, along with custom-made bar stools.

138

Brasserie National

Cascade Chandelier
for Swarovski

2003

Cascade, a table-specific chandelier of vigorous tactile modernity, was designed for Swarovski's Crystal Palace design project. 'When thinking of a chandelier design,' recalls Van Duysen, 'I thought of grand chandeliers, like those in palaces, but mine would evoke a cascading waterfall, which would scatter light and crystals over the table.'

The flowing chains of Swarovski crystals are intermingled with strands of LED lights and allude to the tempestuous swell of water that cascades down a waterfall. The chandelier is a celebration of crystal and light in the grandest sense of the great chandelier tradition.

VDD Residence

Dendermonde, Belgium

1998–2003

The site of this home in Dendermonde is located along the river and is nestled in a group of trees. The house itself is orientated towards the garden, parallel to the river. Along the house's south front, a façade was created with a strong rhythm of solid columns that was inspired by and echoes the planting of the trees, while to the north the house is organized around a patio that acts as a buffer between the street and the building, and allows light to stream into the centre of the structure.

Inside, the columns offer a specific view onto both garden and patio. The vertical circulation divides the house in two, with the kitchen and bathroom to one side, and the living room and bedroom on the other. Typical local building materials have been combined in an abstract palette, from the masonry walls and dark steel window frames to the Belgian bluestone flooring and rough-textured interior plasterwork.

VDD Residence

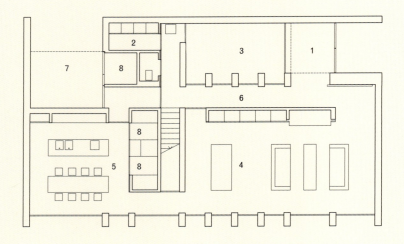

Ground floor

1. Entrance
2. Cloakroom
3. Patio
4. Living room
5. Kitchen
6. Hall
7. Carport
8. Storage room

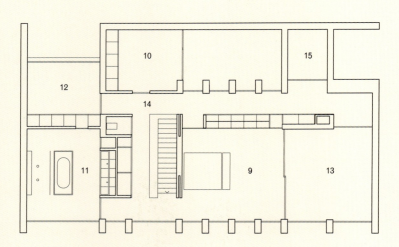

First floor

9. Master bedroom
10. Bedroom
11. Bathroom
12. Dressing room
13. Terrace
14. Night hall
15. Void

VDD Residence

VVD Residence II

Antwerp, Belgium

2001–2003

The classic façade of this 1870 townhouse, a former notaries' office, was restored to its original form and finished with a high-gloss surface. The original floor plan was changed to meet the demands of the new owner, but its typology was retained. On the ground floor, the narrow patio lightens the entry hall, kitchen and dining room; the entry hall opens up onto the large, square living room through an equally large sliding door. The living room itself opens onto the garden with a square pool edged in Belgian bluestone. On the first floor, the spaces are grouped around the TV room, which is painted in charcoal grey and serves as an internal circulation area.

Each of the rooms is noticeable for the lack of ornaments and possessions cluttering up the surfaces. The walls have been finished with an off-white textured plaster that emphasizes the mass, and the doors are treated in the same manner. In the kitchen all attention is drawn towards the huge La Cornue cooker in front of a wall of Delft tiles. All other functional areas can be hidden behind doors.

The original staircase with skylight was kept but simplified to its pure form. The large bedroom with 'library wall' opens up into the bathroom where, as with the cooker in the kitchen, the reclaimed marble bath is the focal point, with the washbasins and shower hidden behind white doors. All fixed lighting is by simple light bulbs, replicas of Thomas Edison's carbon-filament bulbs.

VVD Residence II

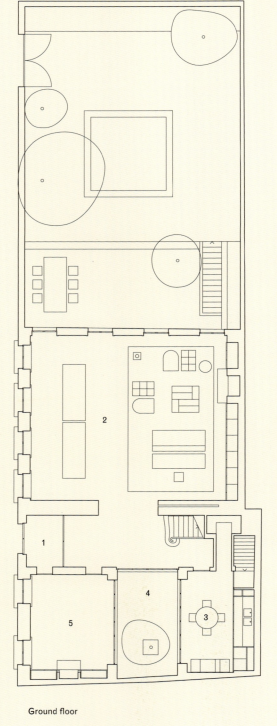
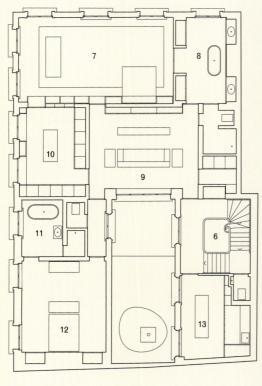

1. Entrance
2. Living room
3. Kitchen
4. Patio
5. Dining area

6. Staircase
7. Master bedroom
8. Master bathroom
9. TV room
10. Dressing room
11. Guest bathroom
12. Guest room
13. Laundry room

Ground floor

First floor

VVD Residence II

VVD Residence II

VVD Residence II

Desk and Chair
for Bulo

2004

Having been challenged by office-furniture firm Bulo to create a compact office system, Van Duysen came up with a design that is a composition of simple planes, referencing both the office landscape that appears in Jacques Tati's film *Play Time* (1967) and the executive furniture of the 1930s, and features smooth edges and a soft colour palette.

The Desk can be configured as an executive desk, a workstation for two or four people, or converted into islands. An extra bookshelf can be added, while the partition panels can be upholstered to reduce noise. The design accommodates both concentration and interaction by offering a choice between high and low partitions, and the overall scheme creates a calm and architectural office environment. With a frame in stainless steel or lacquer, the Chair is a continuation of the design for B&B Italia (see p. 130), and recalls the classic chair designs of Eames. Its pure lines are complemented by the use of innovative materials in the detailing, from the Corian armrests to the ceramic adjustment knobs.

VDE-L Residence

Kortrijk, Belgium
with Pascal Bilquin and Stephanie Laperre

2002–2004

This townhouse, which is situated on an arterial route into Kortrijk, both stands out from and fits in with the more traditional surrounding houses. Built in their style – at least as far as the cornice, the slightly sunken ground floor, and the materials used are concerned – it sits perfectly alongside its neighbours. The construction of the façade guarantees the owners the requisite privacy, with the penthouse on the uppermost floor being set back from the street. The rear of the house may look similar to the front, but its function is completely different. Unlike at the front of the building, here the steel windows are full length.

Whereas most townhouses have a vertically repetitive layout and limited floor space per storey, these problems are avoided through the use of an internal circulation model. The stairwell is not continuous, but is in a different location and runs in a different direction on each floor, creating varying views and perspectives at every turn. This is also a good solution to the problem of the different floor heights. Corridors, too, are introduced to inhibit circulation: built extra-wide, they open up the adjacent rooms or can be used as separate spaces.

The combination of these two approaches mean that vertical circulation is experienced as a stroll through the house, while the use of double-height rooms and avoidance of vertical symmetry in the design of the façade creates interaction between the different floors. The kitchen/living area and outside terrace – all below street level – look onto the garden, which, being level to the street, looks as if it is standing on a platform. The material palette is kept to a strict minimum with masonry walls, dark steel windows and oak flooring.

VDE-L Residence

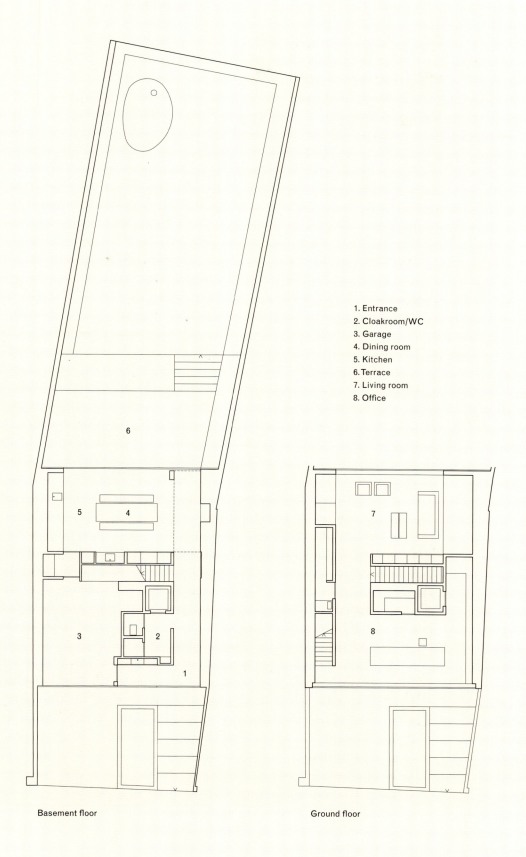

1. Entrance
2. Cloakroom/WC
3. Garage
4. Dining room
5. Kitchen
6. Terrace
7. Living room
8. Office

Basement floor

Ground floor

0   5m

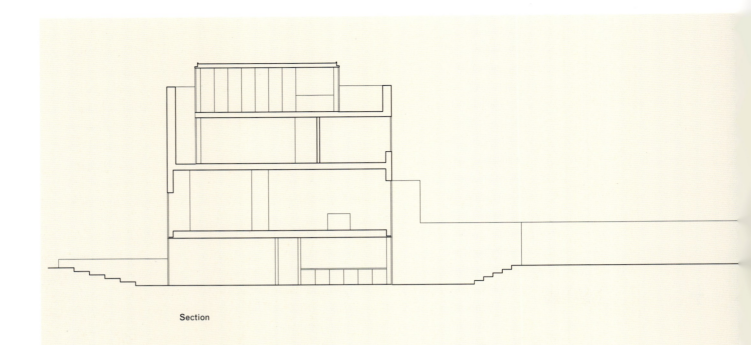

Section

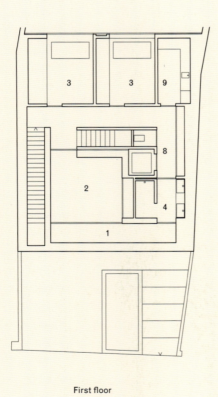

First floor

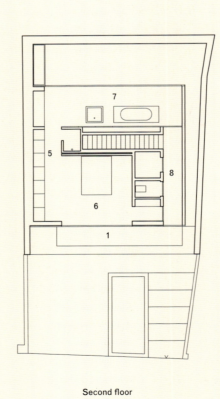

Second floor

1. Terrace
2. Study
3. Bedroom
4. Bathroom
5. Dressing room
6. Master bedroom
7. Master bathroom
8. Night hall
9. Linen room

VDE-L Residence

Pottery Tableware
for When Objects Work

2004

This collection of ceramics for When Objects Work is an exercise in restrained theme and variation. Although each piece can be experienced in isolation, the collection is conceived as an entity, with the differences of scale and colour creating the powerful rhythms and modulations expressed in the subtle yet intense palette of a northern European sea.

Each piece is composed of two elements: an earthenware container and a wooden plate. While the angle of the curve and the smooth profile of each pot are fixed, the diameter and height of the vessels vary; these shifts in scale determine whether the container framed is a bowl or a platter. The thickness of the wooden plate, which serves as both cover and plinth, is also variable.

Serene and sober, these pots have the abstract quality of the archetypal, but they have been pulled from abstraction into the world of physical forms, things you want to touch and to hold. A certain material roughness – the slight irregularities in the surface of the clay, and the soft, weathered grain of the wood – is critical to their character.

Tile Kitchen
for Obumex

2005

With this kitchen for Obumex, Van Duysen has reinterpreted the traditional cooking unit and added a new dimension. The starting point of the design is a tiled block, in which all of the cooking functions are contained. It affords substantial storage, and allows the chef to personalize it by adding a modular cupboard system. The block subtly references the traditional cooking range, while the tiling – in shades of butter yellow, terracotta and moss green – harks back to old-fashioned kitchens where the walls and floors were tiled for hygienic reasons.

The materials and colours of the modular wall unit are determined by the cook's personality, and the block itself can vary from a serene closeness to an open wall unit. The sizing of the tiles according to the modulation of the doors, coupled with the pattern of the joints, ensures that the whole structure retains a plain elegance through highly sophisticated details. This modular system broadens the traditional perception of the range or stove as a piece of furniture intended solely for cooking. The limitations of an ordinary kitchen disappear as the boundaries between range and furniture, kitchen and living room are blurred.

DJ-JVD Residence

Brussels, Belgium

2002–2005

This house, comprising both residence and gallery and encompassing nine floors in total, is situated on a slope between two streets, with two entrances located on different streets. Positioned at the high end of the slope, the house overlooks the gallery – now used for special events for a select audience – and the nearby park. The basement of the house has a roof terrace on top of the gallery, while the first and second floors overlook the city's residential quarter.

Each floor of the house has its own atmosphere. The entrance and basement floor are very light, with white Calacatta marble used extensively for both flooring and furniture, while the second living floor has – despite its white-plastered walls – a much warmer feeling, due to the wall-to-wall carpeting and the clients' collection of furniture. The bedroom floor has a dark and intimate atmosphere, with Golden Brown marble and dark oak panelling. The abstract rear façade, together with its balconies, is in contrast to the more traditional front façade of the house.

184

DJ-JVD Residence

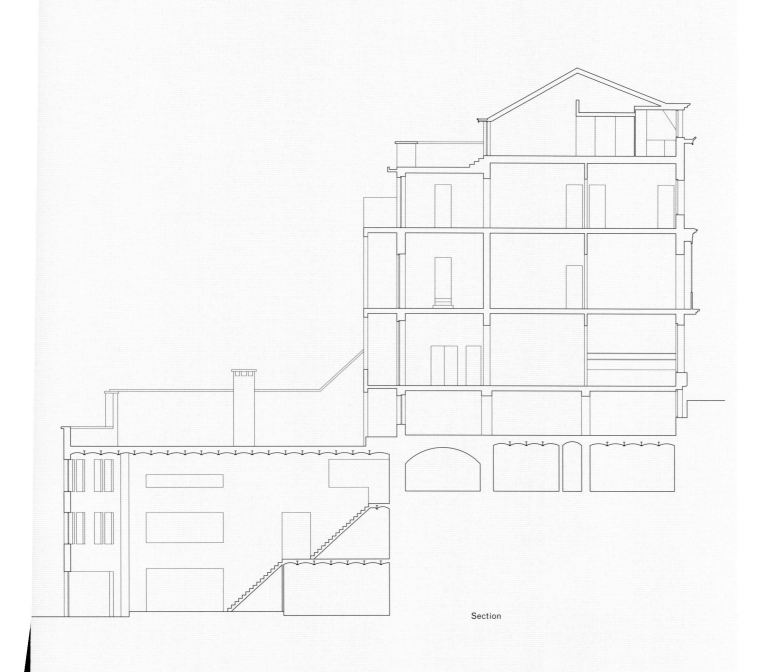

Section

0 ⌞⌞⌞⌞⌞ 5m

DJ-JVD Residence

DJ-JVD Residence

DJ-JVD Residence

Journey up the Hill

I first came across Vincent's work when visiting the Brussels home of James Van Damme and his partner, Dean Johnson. James is a gallerist, and had commissioned from Vincent an architectural intervention on his former gallery, situated at the back of the house. Perched on the top of a hill, this extraordinary building has a deep split section, which means that there is this incredible aspect over the whole of the city. It has a very marked design presence on the landscape.

The house is in an affluent part of Brussels. I remember walking up this wonderfully hilly and leafy street, and turning into what looked like an ordinary turn-of-the-century vernacular building. But upon entering the front door, I was in a space where I was confronted by a particular architectural moment, enveloped in marble. It struck me that this was a transitional system from the outside world to a new world created by Vincent: a world for art, a house created for art lovers.

The distinct transition from the outside to the new space demarcates clear exterior and interior environments. Due to the deep split section of the property, the lower section was utilized in an ingenious way, with the entrances to the house and gallery located on different streets (the house on the higher one, and the gallery on the lower). The new entrance to the house expertly suspends the visitor in anticipation of what is to unfold. Once inside, it is possible to see how Vincent has opened up the house to connect the outside with the inside. He has drawn strong architectural perspectives, which pierce across the building and into the city landscape. This is a very powerful experience, and the morphing of the 19th-century structure provokes questions of perception.

This is architecture of generous proportions. The ground floor is divided into rectangles: the kitchen space and dining space. From here, one sees a new staircase, which leads down to the gallery, and the existing staircase which connects the upper levels. It is at this moment that one understands Vincent's architecture as a new heel for an old house. The structure is made up of a series of walls or galleries, which oscillate between cellular and open-plan systems, always making reference to the view. These spaces act as beautiful backdrops for the works of contemporary art on display.

The new staircase, an amazing structure made of marble, plunges three levels from the living area of the house to the entrance of the gallery. It is here, standing in the staircase, about to enter the main exhibition space, that I realized that this volume is almost twice the size of the existing house. The gallery itself is spread over three levels, with the ground and top floors serving as exhibition spaces, and the office sandwiched in between. The roof forms the garden terrace of the house. The triple-level staircase is lit by a continuous skylight, which presents a second façade inside the building – almost as if the gallery is a house within a house. This façade is an austere set of rectangular apertures, which contain balconies, and its dark colour presents a startling contrast to the traditional front of the house: two very powerful faces inhabiting one form.

   Vincent's design is informed by Modernism, but is highly abstract. It is at the same time relational in terms of use and place, and has the quality of being both present and absent, somehow occupying a space between these two worlds. The use of marble guides one through the building, with the material appearing as entrances, stairs, benches, basins and ledges. This rigour structures the project both intellectually and sensuously.

   Photographs of Vincent's work can only go so far in explaining the intensity and choreography of what he does. He is an architect who makes time, light, space, proportion and nature present.

David Adjaye

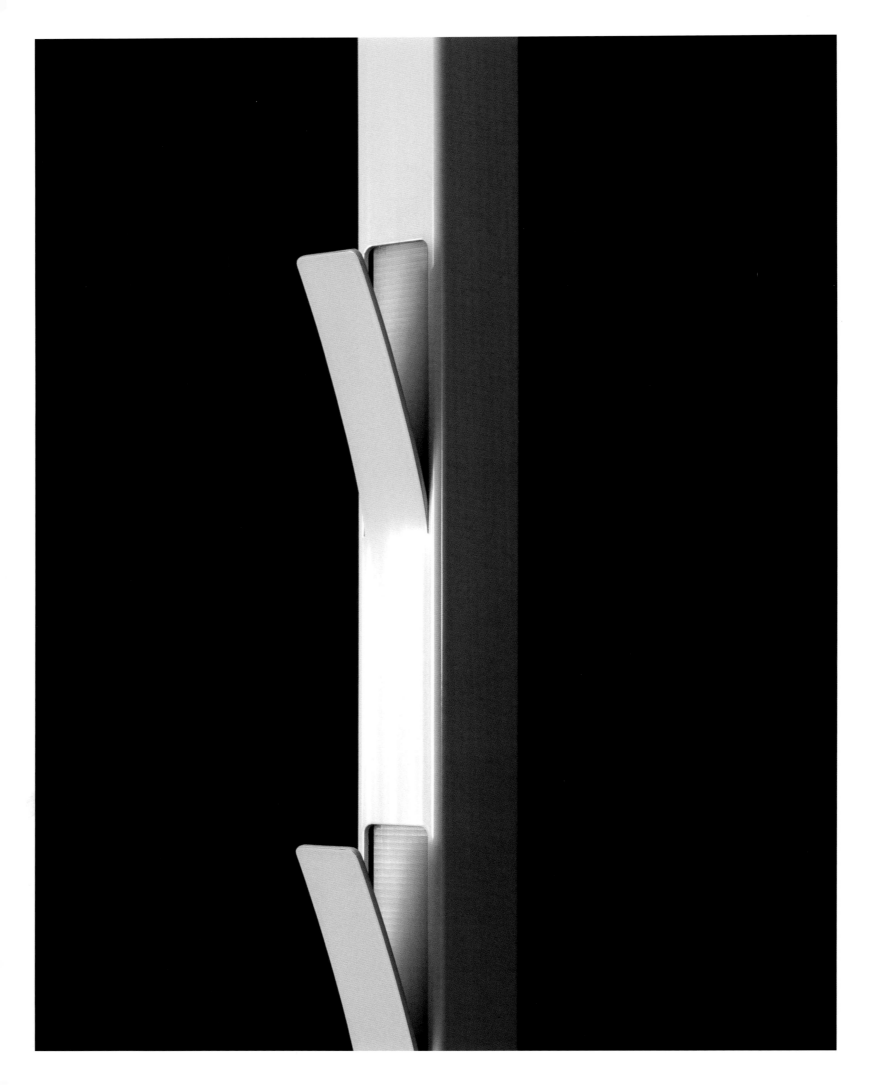

Window Coat Rack
for Viccarbe

2005

This contemporary twist on a traditional hat and clothes rack is available with a complementary umbrella stand, and is fashioned from a gauged lacquered steel tube in thermo-reinforced epoxy, available in black, white or chrome. It can be hung on the wall or leaned against it, or can stand on its own.

The name 'Window' refers to the rounded, laser-cut hooks that 'open' from the steel tube like a window. Their dimensions have been carefully designed to cause the minimum wear and tear on the clothing that is hung on them.

B Residence

Paris, France

2001–2006

This elegant and restrained 1930s townhouse, a modest example of the International Style, is situated in a conservation area of Paris. The brief was to transform the house into a generous, contemporary family home, and any alterations to the original geometric elevations were out of the question. The external envelope, as well as the original winding staircase, has been carefully restored, while the interior has been carved out to both enlarge the volume and open up the plan.

The basement was completely rearranged and enlarged, and part of the garden was dug out to create a *cour anglaise* for the dining room and kitchen, which would provide natural light, fresh air and a terrace for outdoor entertaining. The darker areas at the front of the plan were ideally suited to accommodate an intimate spa facility.

The ground-floor living room is orientated towards a sandstone terrace, whose clean lines complement the rough garden walls and mature trees and shrubbery. A cut-out in the first-floor plate over the living room allows indirect views to the floor above, and lets light filter through between the two spaces. All of the upper floors are dedicated to sleeping and studying, with the master bedroom facilities occupying the entire first floor. The roof has been extended with a small volume to house the staircase, lift and services, with the remaining area turned into a large, sunny roof terrace.

Although the treatment of the new surfaces is resolutely contemporary, the manners, materials and colours of this extensive refurbishment have remained very close to the original atmosphere. The pure whiteness of the walls is only interrupted now and then by the slimline black metal frames of the new windows, the dark-stained panelled walls and furniture, the grey-white marble of the bathrooms, and the grey Indian stone and stainless steel of the kitchen. This house has been restored and transformed, and has only gained in elegance, style, and a certain smooth charm.

Rear elevation

Front elevation

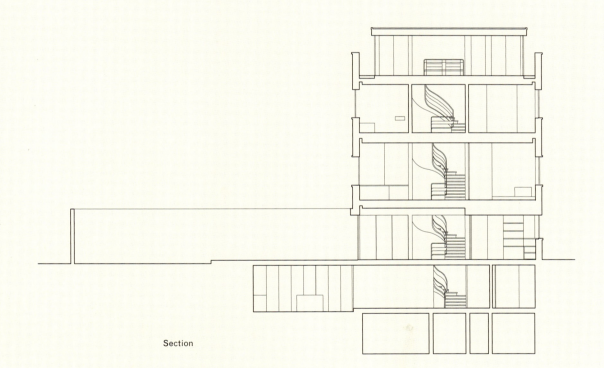

Section

0 |____|____|____|____|____| 5m

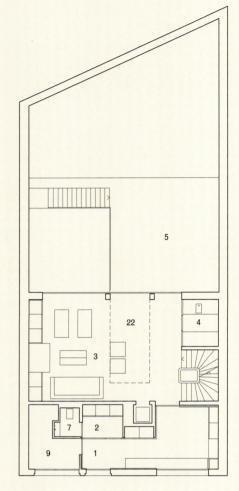

Ground floor

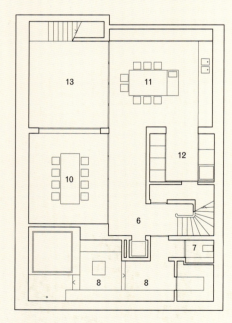

Basement floor

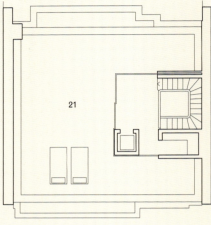

Third floor

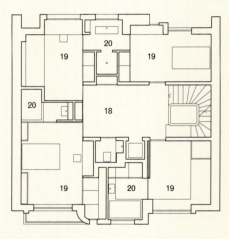

Second floor

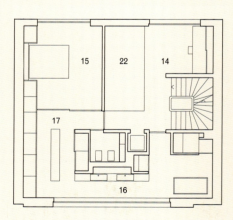

First floor

1. Entrance
2. Cloakroom/WC
3. Living room
4. Bar
5. Terrace
6. Hall
7. WC
8. Spa + facilities
9. Storage room
10. Dining room
11. Kitchen
12. Kitchen pantry
13. Patio
14. Office
15. Master bedroom
16. Master bathroom
17. Dressing room
18. Night hall
19. Room
20. Bathroom
21. Roof terrace
22. Void

B Residence

Green Ribbon Light Fixture
for DAB

2006

This collection for Spanish lighting firm DAB was created with a strong, architectural background. The geometric forms of the fixtures find their roots in the typology of Constructivism, and are reminiscent of the basic language of early Modernist sculpture. Materials are kept to a minimum, with only aluminium and bronze used to enhance the pure, graphic design. Only one colour accent interferes with the monochromatic materials: a green ribbon which lightens up the design of the light fixture.

Private Residence

Antwerp, Belgium

2003–2007

The renovation and extension of this early 20th-century building, located on the edge of the city centre and overlooking the River Scheldt and the container ships slowly making their way in and out of the harbour, was commissioned by a private client who wanted to transform the two upper floors into office spaces and create a three-storey penthouse on top. Considering the technical limitations of the site, this looked set to be a challenging task for the building team. And as it was necessary that the ground and first floors were able to continue functioning throughout the construction process, the design became even more complex.

In order to bear the extra weight of the extension, the foundations had to be consolidated. Given the restrictions in the load capacity of the existing building's concrete columns and beams, special measures had to be taken to minimize the weight of the additional storeys. A steel construction of columns and beams, dimensioned according to the grid of the concrete structure, was placed and assembled on top of the building. Measures to reduce the additional load brought upon the structure included making floors out of I-shaped wood beams, covering structural walls with plasterboard, and fashioning honeycomb plates that supported thin layers of stone.

The spatial organization of the three-storey penthouse was structured by a rectangular void that perforated the two dividing floors within the axes of the horizontal grid and shifted along its vertical axes. Closed boxes housing specific living functions were placed between the floor slabs. According to their use and spatial appearance, they were covered with different materials such as glass, wood, stone and plasterboard. Due to the open-plan and perforated floor levels, the dwelling achieves an unusual and special character.

Private Residence

Front elevation

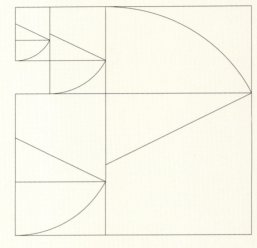

Elevation scheme

1. Technical room
2. Entrance hall
3. Staircase
4. Fitness room
5. Guest room
6. Bathroom
7. Terrace
8. WC
9. Living room
10. Dining room
11. Kitchen
12. Storage
13. Void
14. Bedroom
15. Dressing room
16. Roof garden

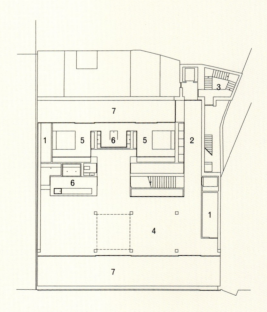

Fourth floor

214

Private Residence

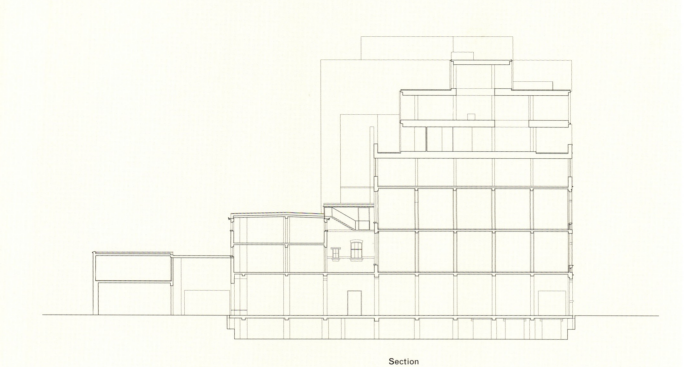

Section

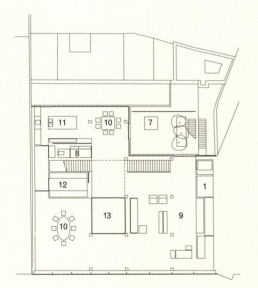

Fifth floor

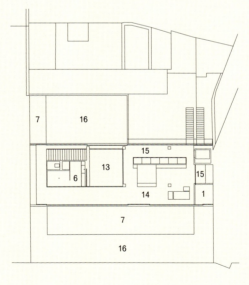

Sixth floor

0 ⌊____⌊____⌊ 10m

Gaston Chair
for Poliform

2008

The Gaston Chair, created for furniture company Poliform, was designed with both exclusivity and refinement in mind. It is structured in varnished metal, in white or black, with the seat and back cushions filled with feather and polyurethane foam of different densities and covered in a cotton cloth. Removable covers are available in both fabric and soft leather. The elegant lines more than live up to the chair's gentlemanly name.

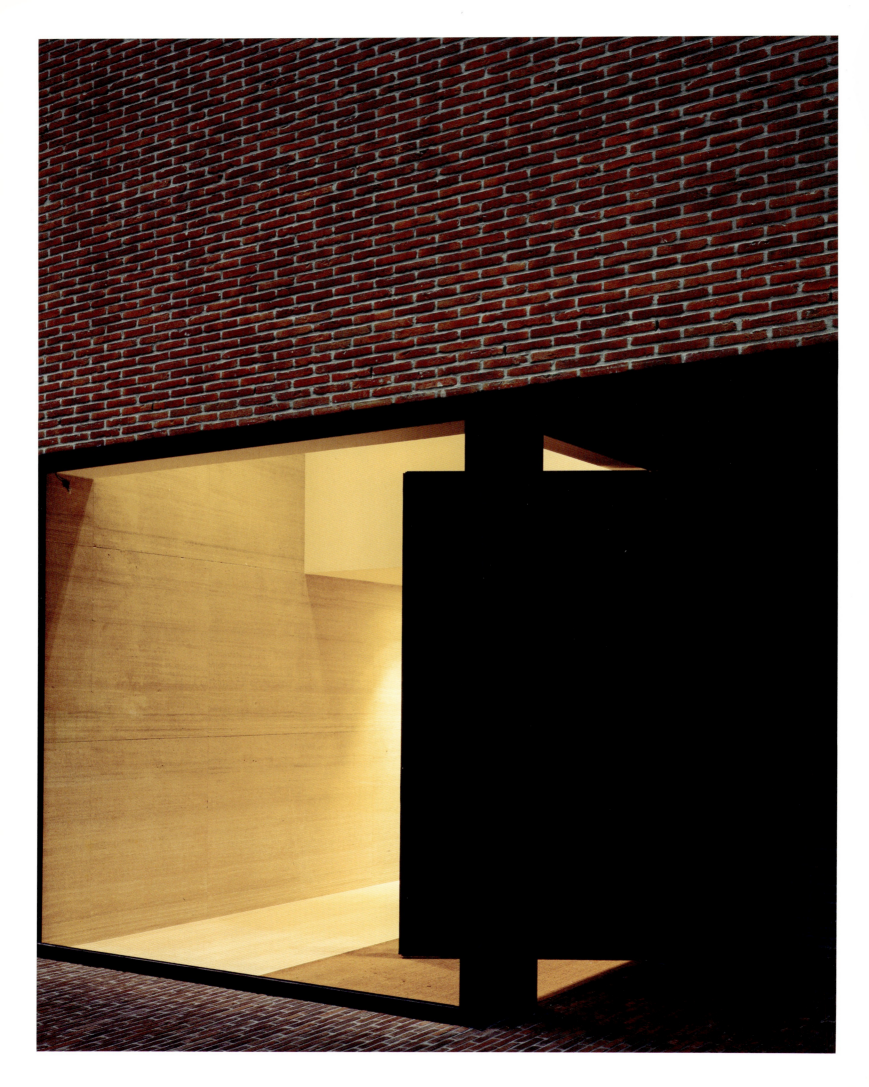

VDV-G Residence

Zonhoven, Belgium

1999–2008

The use of local red brick in this family home could be seen as an attempt to allow the house to blend into the typically Flemish suburban street. But if the choice of external material is traditional, the materials used for the internal surfaces – travertine and walnut – not to mention the geometry and complexity of the layout, are not.

The house consists of two stacked volumes that have been moved slightly off-centre from each other. The plan is organized around two axes that form a cross: the first axis starts from the entrance hall and allows a view to the other side of the site, while the second runs back to front between the two staircases, connecting the formal rooms at the front with the family rooms at the back. Natural light is pulled in via one large window and several patios; only the rear elevation opens up fully to the landscape beyond. The organization of the house is otherwise quite traditional, accentuating the circulation areas with double-height ceilings and indirect natural light.

224

VDV-G Residence

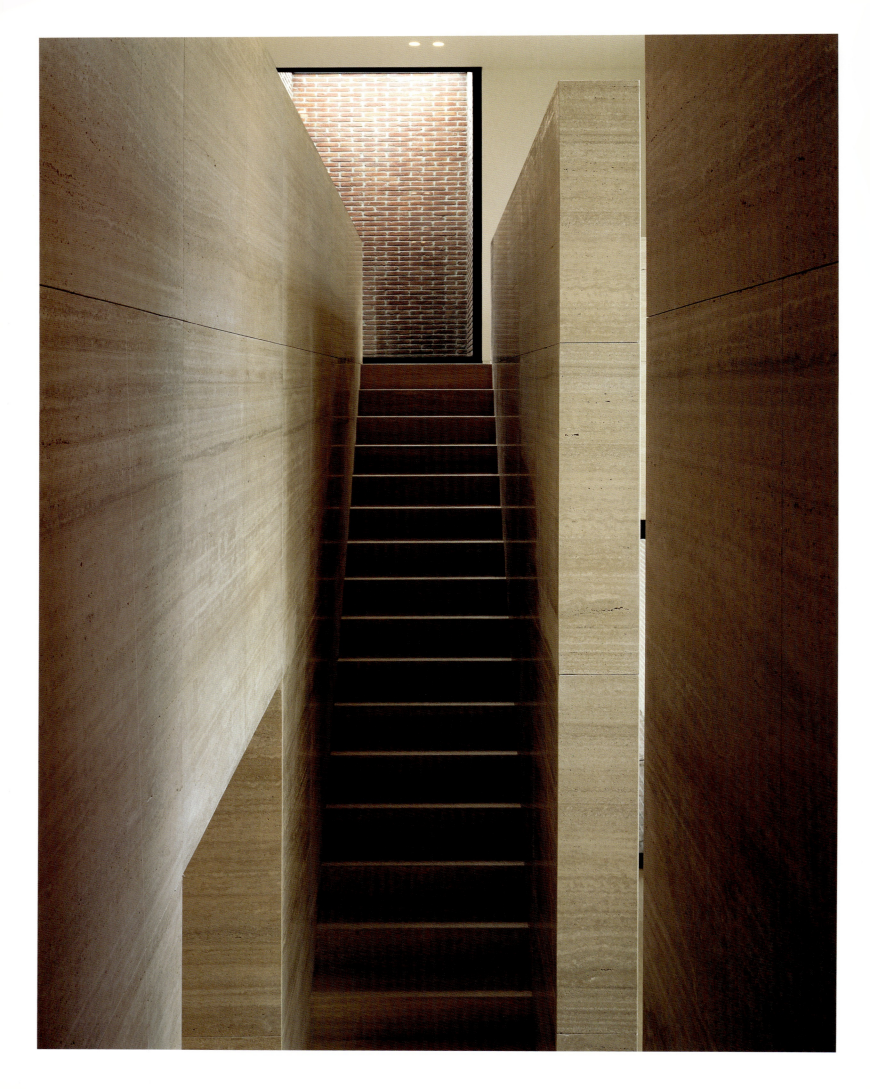

VDV-G Residence

VDV-G Residence

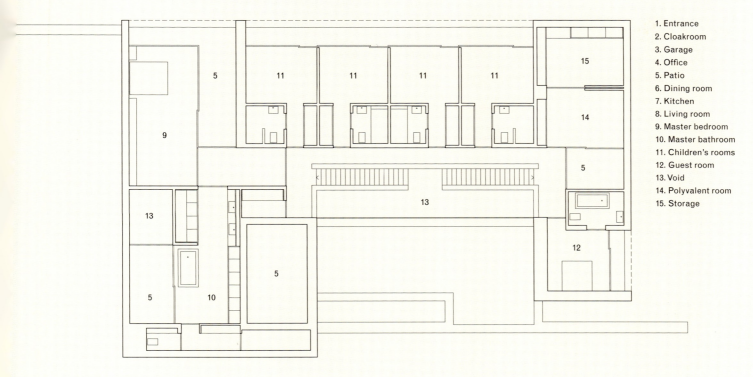

First floor

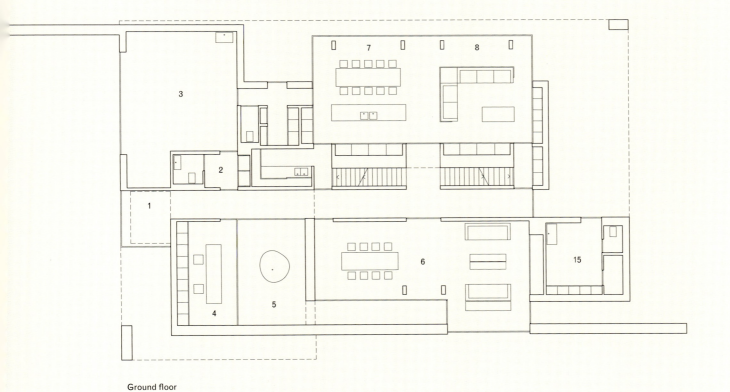

Ground floor

1. Entrance
2. Cloakroom
3. Garage
4. Office
5. Patio
6. Dining room
7. Kitchen
8. Living room
9. Master bedroom
10. Master bathroom
11. Children's rooms
12. Guest room
13. Void
14. Polyvalent room
15. Storage

0 — 5m

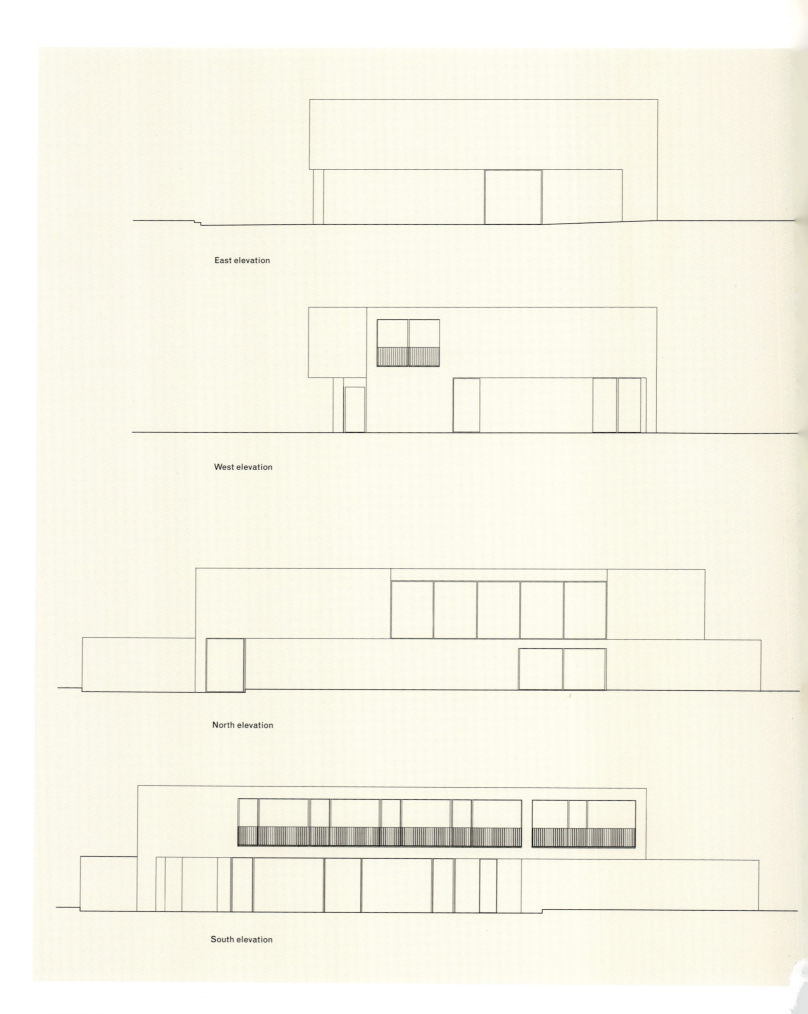

East elevation

West elevation

North elevation

South elevation

VDV-G Residence

S Residential Complex

Antwerp, Belgium

2002–2008

This project is a prime example of urban regeneration. A derelict auction room, neglected for the last ten years, and some of its surrounding buildings were acquired with the intention of reviving and 'unlocking' a patch of urban fabric in the historic centre of Antwerp. The site occupied a T-shaped piece of land, containing two buildings with street elevations and the large volume of the Art Deco auction room, placed almost centrally within the plan. Although the former contained period features that at first glance seemed to be in adequate condition, the reality turned out to be a bit different and a new build was proposed.

The original roof over the large auction space, which previously had a greenhouse-type skylight and a semi-translucent inner skin, has been replaced with a steel-and-glass roof that allows a view of the sky. The enclosed garden connecting the four parts of the project was landscaped to provide easy and elegant access to the auction-room volume, the block of 'landlocked' apartments at the rear of the site, and the underground parking facilities for the owners.

The premises in the Leopoldstraat, a stone's throw from the Antwerp Botanic Garden, were transformed into contemporary loft apartments with glazed elevations and large, L-shaped terraces at the rear. The ground floor has been turned into a commercial space, with the possibility of using the auction room as a showroom. The existing derelict building in Van Heurckstraat made way for new lofts, too, again opening up with terraces to the inner courtyard. Both buildings feature open-plan layouts for the lofts, with uninterrupted views from front to back, and rooftop apartments with generous, sunny terraces.

The language of this project is resolutely urban and restrained, using a very hard, dark brick for the street elevations, and windows and balconies in black steel and toughened glass at the more private courtyard side.

S Residential Complex

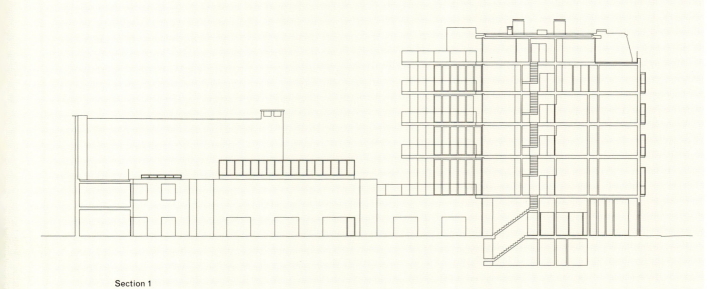

Section 1

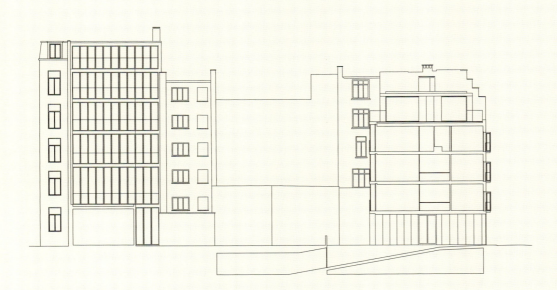

Section 2

Fourth floor　　First–third floors

Front elevation 1

Front elevation 2

238

S Residential Complex

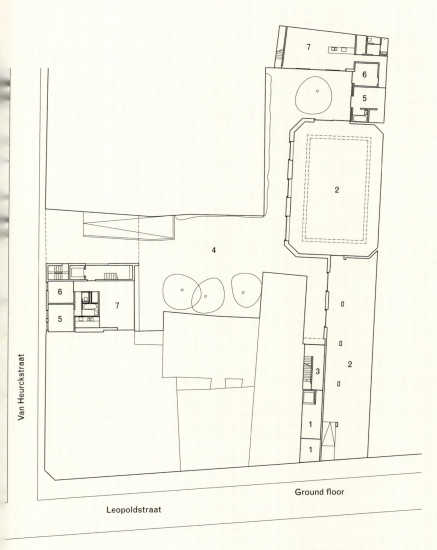
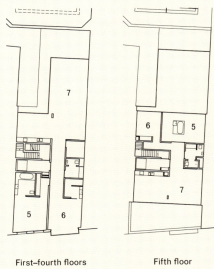

Ground floor First–fourth floors Fifth floor

Leopoldstraat

Van Heurckstraat

1. Entrance apartments
2. Commercial space
3. Staircase
4. Inner courtyard
5. Master bedroom
6. Bedroom
7. Living area

0 — 10m

Neutra Outdoor Collection
for Tribù

2008

The Neutra Outdoor Collection for Belgian furniture company Tribù, consisting of an armchair, an easy chair and a lounger, together with two accessory tables, is a timeless line of sober elegance, discreet luxury and well-considered detailing. This elegance finds expression in the clean, simple forms and restrained style, complemented by an assured sense of detail. The main shell of the chairs and lounger is available in lacquered plywood or Batyline textile; the triangular frame is created through an injected aluminium technique; while the armrests have a matte-black inlay.

Chronology

D Residence, Waasmunster, Belgium, 1990

VVD Residence 1, Antwerp, Belgium, 1993
page 24

AK Residence, Antwerp, Belgium, 1994
page 28

DB-VB Residence, Mol, Belgium, 1993–1994

Simple d'Anvers Shop, Antwerp, Belgium, 1994

Natan Shop, Brussels, Belgium, 1995–1996
page 36

Ars et Labor Showroom, Zele, Belgium, 1996

Copyright Bookshop, Antwerp, Belgium, 1996

VN Residence, Waasmunster, Belgium, 1994–1997

Chronology

DB-VD Residence, Sint-Amandsberg, Belgium, 1994–1997
page 40

M Residence, Mallorca, Spain, 1996–1997
page 42

JVD Gallery, Brussels, Belgium, 1996–1997

VH Residence, Lokeren, Belgium, 1995–1998
page 48

V Residence, Brussels, Belgium, 1997–1998
page 54

VD Residence, Wilrijk, Belgium, 1995–1998

De Plantaardige Verbeelding Shop, Antwerp, Belgium, 1997–1998

VD Residence, Lochristi, Belgium, 1998

BACOB Offices, Kalmthout / Brasschaat / Kapellen / Mol / Geel, Belgium, 1996–1999

M-R Residence, Brussels, Belgium, 1998–1999

RA Residence, Antwerp, Belgium, 1998–1999

Xandres Shop, Brussels / Ghent / Knokke, Belgium; Lille, France, 1998–1999

M Pavilion, Arendonk, Belgium, 1999

Sportmax Shop, Milan, Italy; Paris, France; Tokyo, Japan 1999; *page 64*

RH-BH Residence, New York, USA, 1999
page 68

Wash Basin for Obumex, 1999
page 74

Fashion Club, Antwerp, Belgium, 1998–1999
page 76

Concordia Offices, Waregem, Belgium, 1998–2000
page 80

Hampton Bays Shop, Brussels / Ghent / Knokke / Antwerp, Belgium, 1998–2000

VL Residence, Bruges, Belgium, 1999–2000
page 90

Dany May Shop, Antwerp, Belgium, 2000

Selfridges Womenswear Floor, London, UK, 2000

Natan Shop, Brussels, Belgium, 2000

Capco Offices, Edegem, Belgium, 2000

Beam Light Fixture for Modular, 2000

DC Residence, Waasmunster, Belgium, 1998–2001
page 94

M Residence, Lier, Belgium, 1998–2001

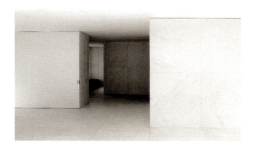

M-VS Residence, Brussels, Belgium, 1999–2001
page 108

Capco Offices, Antwerp, Belgium; New York, USA; San Francisco, USA; Singapore, 1999–2001; *page 120*

P-I Residence, Kortrijk, Belgium, 1999–2001

D Residence, Knokke, Belgium, 2000–2001

EV Residence, Brussels, Belgium, 2000–2001

P Residence, Antwerp, Belgium, 2000–2001

G-VM Residence, Wilrijk, Belgium, 2000–2001

Copyright Bookshop, Antwerp, Belgium, 2000–2001
page 124

M Housing Complex, Hamburg, Germany, 2001

VO-I Residence, Antwerp, Belgium, 2000–2001

Nido Chair for Cappellini, 2000–2001

VVD Collection for B&B Italia, 2002
page 130

DR Residence, Boechout, Belgium, 1999–2002
page 132

Brasserie National, Antwerp, Belgium, 2000–2002
page 136

Selfridges Menswear Floor, Manchester, UK, 2001–2002

B Residence, New York, USA, 2002

IC Residence, London, UK, 2001–2002

Turnover Shop, Antwerp, Belgium, 2002

A-VH Offices, Antwerp, Belgium, 2002

Tea Rose Shop, Monza, Italy, 2000–2002

Tea Rose Café, Monza, Italy, 2002

DN Residence, Waasmunster, Belgium, 2001–2002

Cascade Chandelier for Swarovski, 2003
page 142

VDD Residence, Dendermonde, Belgium, 1998–2003
page 144

VVD Residence 11, Antwerp, Belgium, 2001–2003
page 154

N-J Residence, Hattem, Netherlands, 2001–2003

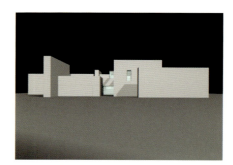

V Residence, Kortrijk, Belgium, 2003

Chronology

L Residence, Antwerp, Belgium, 2002–2003

M·B Residence, Dessel, Belgium, 2001–2004

School for Product Design (competition), Kortrijk, Belgium, 2004

G·VD Residence, Knokke, Belgium, 2002–2004

VL Medical Practice, Antwerp, Belgium, 2004

Inbev lobby, café, restaurant and offices (competition), Leuven, Belgium, 2003–2004

Desk and Chair for Bulo, 2004
page 170

VDE-L Residence, Kortrijk, Belgium, 2002–2004
with Pascal Bilquin and Stephanie Laperre
page 172

Residence for the Elderly (competition), Lede, Belgium, 2004

Private Office, Antwerp, Belgium, 2003–2004

Crematorium (competition), Sint-Niklaas, Belgium, 2004

Pottery Tableware for When Objects Work, 2004
page 178

Chronology

Tile Kitchen for Obumex, 2005
page 180

DJ-JVD Residence, Brussels, Belgium, 2002–2005
page 182

Antwerp Tower Lobby, Antwerp, Belgium, 2004–2005

Emporio Armani Shop (concept), London, UK, 2005

F Residence, Isle-sur-la-Sorgue, France, 2005

Window Coat Rack for Viccarbe, 2005
page 194

Martyr's Square (competition), Beirut, Lebanon, 2005
with Nabil Gholam Architecture and Vladimir Djurovic Landscape Architecture

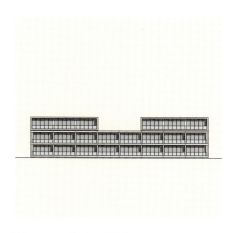

R Apartments, Boechout, Belgium, 2005

B Residence, Paris, France, 2001–2006
page 196

Block 20-02, Beirut, Lebanon, 2006

TM-DW Residence, The Hague, Netherlands, 2004–2006

Green Ribbon Light Fixture for DAB, 2006
page 204

VB-VH Residence, Knokke, Belgium, 2005–2006

VD-H Residence, Lokeren, Belgium, 2005–2006

Chronology

Home Kitchen for Varenna, 2006

Belgian Bluestone Stand, Interieur 06, Kortrijk, Belgium, 2006

Private Residence, Antwerp, Belgium, 2003–2007
page 206

Anemonen Housing Project (competition), Tienen, Belgium, 2007

V Residence, Kortrijk, Belgium, 2003–2007

D-M Residence, Knokke, Belgium, 2005–2007

Atelier Table for Home St Paul, 2007

L Residence, Antwerp, Belgium, 2007

EB-GM Residence, Valencia, Spain, 2007

Gaston Chair for Poliform, 2008
page 218

VDV-G Residence, Zonhoven, Belgium, 1999–2008
page 220

S Residential Complex, Antwerp, Belgium, 2002–2008
page 234

Chronology

Hotel Ergo, Antwerp, Belgium, 2004–2008

DN Residence, Wilrijk, Belgium, 2004–2008

L Residence, Sint-Martens-Latem, Belgium, 2005–2008

Oberon Door Handle for Valli & Valli, 2006–2008

H Residence, Knokke, Belgium, 2007–2008

Belgian Bluestone Stand, Interieur 08, Kortrijk, Belgium, 2008

Neutra Outdoor Collection for Tribù, 2008
page 242

Primitives Tableware for When Objects Work, 2008

Valentino Shop (competition), Milan, Italy, 2008

Tour & Taxis Reception Desk, Brussels, Belgium, 2007–2008

TV Stand for Luke Furniture, 2008

A Residential Complex, Antwerp, Belgium, 2003–2009

KI Residential Complex, Ghent, Belgium, 2004–2009

MR Residence, Milan, Italy, 2005–2009

T Residence, Waasmunster, Belgium, 2005–2009

S Residence, Deurle, Belgium, 2005–2009

VH-DL Residence, Knokke, Belgium, 2005–2009

V Residence, Lummen, Belgium, 2005–2009

S Residence, Zwolle, Netherlands, 2006–2009

H·U Residence, London, UK, 2007–2009

Graanmarkt 13 Shop, Antwerp, Belgium, 2007–2009

B Residence, Zwevegem, Belgium, 2006–2009

V·DC Residence, Buggenhout, Belgium, 2004–2009

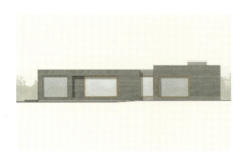

L Residence, Aalst, Belgium, 2005–2009

Van Loock Shop, Zandhoven, Belgium, 2005–2009

Arthur & Fox Shop, Paris, France, 2007–2009

La Rinascente Womenswear Floor, Milan / Padova / Palermo, Italy, 2007–2009

Dry Tile for Brix, 2008–2009

Café l'Officiel, Scènes d'intérieur, Maison et Objet, Paris, France, 2009

V Residence, Tessenderlo, Belgium, 2004–2010

VDV Residence, Hove, Belgium, 2010

DC Residence, Tielrode, Belgium, 2006–2010

M-VDV Residence, Sint-Niklaas, Belgium, 2005–2010

VDC Residence, Kortrijk, Belgium, 2005–2010

V-M Residence, Sint-Martens-Latem, Belgium, 2007–2010

W Residence, Knokke, Belgium, 2006–2010

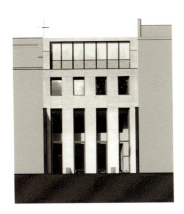

V Residence, Brussels, Belgium, 2007–2010

T-R Residence, Knokke, Belgium, 2008–2010

DL Residence, Kruishoutem, Belgium, 2009–2011

P Residence, Oostduinkerke, Belgium, 2008–2010

Youth Hostel (competition), Antwerp, Belgium, 2004–2010

Chronology

BAS Residence (preliminary design), Dubai, UAE, 2007–
in collaboration with Vladimir Djurovic Landscape Architecture

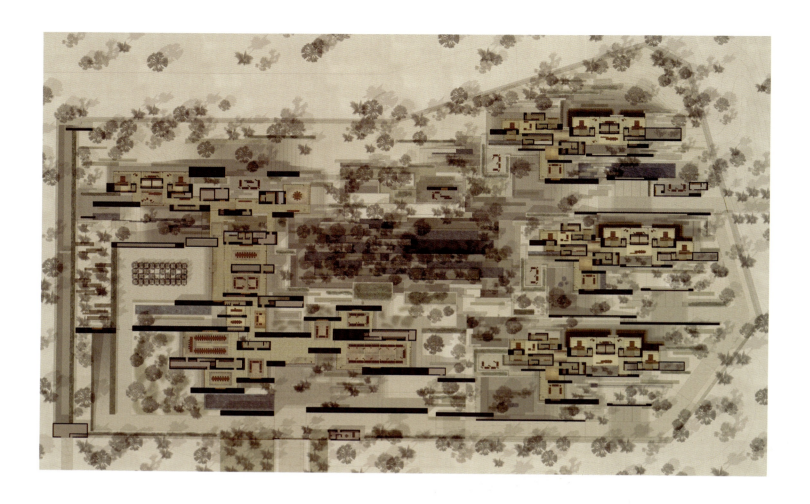

BAS Residence (preliminary design), Dubai, UAE, 2007–
in collaboration with Vladimir Djurovic Landscape Architecture

Residential Tower, Jeddah, Saudi Arabia, 2008–

Chronology

Design Team

Wouter Bastijns
Pascal Bilquin
Mathias Blonde
Johan Buelens
David Bulckaen
Daphne Daskal
Lies De Baere
Joep Debie
Amaury De Valensart
Liesbet De Vis
Brigitte D'hoore
Marleen Frimout
Kristof Geldmeyer
Christine Gerlach
Ann Goossens
Bart Goossens
Cedric Illegems
Sophie Laenen
Stephanie Laperre
Peter Lefebre
Pieter Maes
Sophie Meersseman
Marc Merckx
Steven Milliau
Humberto Nóbrega

Bruno Peeters
Kristina Potvlieghe
Stijn Rolies
Dat Schöffner
Filip Schöning
Nicolas Schuybroek
Dominik Schwarzer
Glenn Sestig
Patricia Sipido
Hans Sterck
Carl Stragier
Sönke Timm
Bert Van Boxelaere
Liesbet Vandenbussche
Natalie Vanderick
Jan Van Gassen
Elke Van Goel
Matthias Van Halewyck
Lene Van Look
Hanne Van Reusel
Annemarie Van Riet
Stein Van Rossem
Hans Verstuyft
Peter Vlaminck

Personal Assistants
Sybil Barsamian
Carine Goossens
Marianne Swyzen
Dotty Van Puyvelde

Bibliography

100 Architecture Competition Works (LST Publishing House, Shenyang, 2009).

ADI Design Index (Associazione per il Disegno Industriale, Milan, 2003).

Alejandro Bahamon, *Sketch, Plan, Build: World Class Architects Show How It's Done* (Harper Design International, New York, 2005).

Franco Bertoni, *Minimalist Design* (Birkhäuser, Basel, 2004).

Lise Coirier, ed., *Label-Design.be* (Stichting Kunstboek, Oostkamp, 2005).

Liliane Knopes, ed., *Belgium New Architecture*, vols. 2 and 3 (Prisme Editions, Brussels, 2003 and 2005).

Luxury Houses: Top of the World (TeNeues, New York, 2008).

Javier Rodriguez Marcos and Anatxu Zabalbeascoa, *Minimalisms: A Sign of the Times* (Gustavo Gili, Barcelona, 2000).

Virginia McLeod, *Detail in Contemporary Bathroom Design* (Laurence King, London, 2009).

Emma O'Kelly and Corinna Dean, *Conversions* (Laurence King, London, 2007).

Wim Pauwels, *Hedendaags wonen in België* (Beta-Plus, Enghien, 2005).

———, *Living with Colour* (Beta-Plus, Enghien, 2006).

Phyllis Richardson, *House Plus* (Thames & Hudson, London, 2005).

Angelika Taschen, ed., *Brussels Style* (Taschen, Cologne, 2006).

———, *Nouveaux intérieurs de la côte* (Taschen, Cologne, 2008).

The Phaidon Atlas of Contemporary Townhouses (Phaidon, London, 2008).

Jessica Cargill Thompson, *40 Under 40: Young Architects for the New Millennium* (Taschen, Cologne, 2000).

Suzanne Trocme, *Attention to Detail* (Jacqui Small, London, 2004).

Marcel Wanders, ed., *The International Design Yearbook* (Laurence King, London, 2005).

World Architecture and Interiors (Beta-Plus, Enghien, 2005).

Vincent Van Duysen (Gustavo Gili, Barcelona, 2001).

Yearbook Architecture Flanders (Flemish Architecture Institute, Antwerp, 1996, 1998, 2002).

Awards

Charles Wilford Award 1994
 DB-VD Residence
Arch & Life, Belgian European Architectural Awards 1995
 Honourable citation
Outstanding Young Persons Award 1999 *Laureate, personal developments and realizations*
Awards van de Belgische Architectuur
 2001 *Concordia Offices*
 2002 *DC Residence*
ADI Design Index 2003
 VVD Collection, B&B Italia
4-Yearly Provincial Prize for Architecture of the Province West-Flanders 2003 *Concordia Offices*
Henry Van de Velde Prize 2004
 Pottery Tableware, When Objects Work
Maison & Objet, Scènes d'intérieur 2009 *Designer of the year*

Exhibitions

Salone del Mobile, Milan, 1988, 1999, 2000, 2002, 2003, 2004, 2005, 2006, 2008, 2009.

'Mein erstes Haus', deSingel International Artcenter, Antwerp and De Brakke Grond, Amsterdam, January 1994.

'Nouvelle Architecture en Flandre', Centre d'architecture Arc-en-Rêve, Bordeaux, 1996.

'100 Jaar, 100 Stoelen', Design Museum, Ghent, 21 June–15 September 2002.

'Somewhere Totally Else: The European Design Show', Design Museum, London, 26 September 2003–4 January 2004.

Interieur Biennale, Kortrijk, 2004, 2008.

Design Week, Munich, 2004.

'Design from Flanders', Melbourne Museum, 2004.

Swarovski Crystal Palace collection, Shanghai Arts Festival, 2004; Marshall Field's, Chicago, 2005; Paris Theater, Miami, 2005; Paris, 2005.

'Glamour', San Francisco Museum of Modern Art, 9 October 2004–17 January 2005.

'(Im)perfect by Design', Koninklijke Musea voor Kunst en Geschiedenis, Brussels, 3 December 2004–17 February 2005.

'Label-Design.be: Design in Belgium After 2000', Musée du Grand-Hornu, Hornu, 16 October 2005–16 February 2006.

'New Design from Flanders', Design Centre of the Czech Republic, Prague, 14 October–11 November 2005 and Design Centre, Brno, 24 November 2005–8 January 2006.

Philadelphia Museum of Art, 2006.

Moss Gallery, New York, 2006.

VIA/Design Yearbook Exhibition, Paris, 2006.

'Classic', Kortrijk, 2006.

The Moscow World Fine Art Fair, 2006.

'Design de Flandre', Montreal, 14 September–22 October 2006.

'Nieuwe Belgische Vormgeving', Museum Waterland, Pummerend, 18 May–24 June 2007.

'Dag van de Architectuur, Interieur Foundation, Kortrijk, 14 October 2007.

'5e Triënnale voor Vormgeving', Koninklijke Musea voor Kunst Geschiedenis, Brussels, 14 December 2007–2 March 2008.

'New and Norwegian: A World of Folk', Stavanger 2008, Gravarsveien, Sandnes, 5 July–5 October 2008.

Maison & Objet, Paris, 2009.

Photo credits

Every effort has been made to trace the copyright owners of the images contained in this book and we apologize for any unintentional omissions. We would be pleased to insert an appropriate acknowledgment in any reprint of this publication.

All photographs by Alberto Piovano, except for the following:

4, 6 (top), 24, 25, 49, 50, 155–63, 165–69, 251 (bottom row, centre) Martyn Thompson; 6 (bottom), 91 Andrea Ferrari; 7 Manolo Yllera; 8 Willy Vanderperre; 12 (top), 15 (bottom), 16, 17 (top), 20–21, 77, 92, 93, 118–19, 126, 128–29, 247 (middle row, centre), 247 (bottom row, centre and right), 249 (bottom row, centre), 250 (top row, left), 252 (middle row, right), 255 (top row, centre), 256 (bottom row, centre), 257 (top row, centre), 258 (top row, centre), 259 (middle row, right) Koen Van Damme; 13, 18, 249 (middle row, right), 250 (bottom row, left and right), 251 (bottom row, left), 252 (top row, left), 252 (bottom row, right), 253 (top row, right), 253 (middle row, right), 254 (top row, right), 254 (middle row, left and centre), 254 (bottom row, left), 255 (middle row, left), 255 (bottom row, left and right), 257 (middle row, right), 257 (bottom row, left and right), 258 (middle row, left and right), 259 (bottom row, right), 260 (middle row, centre and right), 260 (bottom row, left), 261 (top row, right), 261 (middle row, left and centre), 261 (bottom row, left and right), 262 (middle row, all), 262 (bottom row, all), 263 (top), 263 (middle row, left), 263 (bottom row, all), 264 (all), 265 (all), 266 (all), 267 (top row, left and right) Vincent Van Duysen Architects; 19 (bottom), 254 (top row, left) Kristien Daem/Bulo; 26–27, 110 Giorgio Possenti; 66 Sportmax; 70 (left), 73, 108, 117 Jean-Luc Laloux; 70–71, 72, 246 (top row, centre) José Van Riele; 82, 246 (bottom row, left) Guido Van Duysen; 133 Didier Delmas; 142, 252 (middle row, centre) Swarovski; 186, 187, 189 Christoph Kicherer; 246 (top row, right), 246 (middle row, left) Verne; 246 (middle row, centre) Marcel Gruyaert; 247 (middle row, right), 250 (middle row, right), 251 (top row, left) Jan Verlinde; 248 (top row, right) Xandres; 248 (middle row, left) J. P. Gabriel; 249 (top row, left) Hampton Bays; 249 (top row, centre) Tim Van de Velde; 249 (top row, right) Dany May; 249 (middle row, left), 251 (middle row, right) Selfridges; 249 (middle row, centre) Natan; 249 (bottom row, left) Modular; 249 (bottom row, right) Sarah Blee; 250 (middle row, left), 253 (bottom row, right), 255 (middle row, centre) Marc Merckx; 250 (middle row, centre) Jo Pauwels; 251 (top row, centre) Cappellini; 251 (top row, right) B&B Italia; 251 (bottom row, right) Misha De Ridder/Turnover; 252 (top row, centre and right) Tea Rose; 252 (middle row, left) Descamps; 252 (bottom row, left and centre), 259 (middle row, centre), 261 (top row, left) Vincent Van Duysen; 253 (middle row, left), 260 (bottom row, centre) Jan Van Gassen; 253 (bottom row, left), 256 (middle row, right), 260 (bottom row, right), 261 (top row, centre) Kristof Geldmeyer; 253 (bottom row, centre) Laurent Boeki; 254 (bottom row, right), 259 (bottom row, centre) When Objects Work; 255 (top row, right), 256 (bottom row, right), 259 (top row, all), 260 (top row, left and right), 261 (middle row, right), 261 (bottom row, centre) Stijn Rolies; 255 (middle row, right) Viccarbe; 256 (top row, left and centre), 256 (middle row, left), 268 (all) Pixelab; 256 (bottom row, left) DAB; 257 (top row, left) Varenna; 258 (top row, left) Filip Vereecke; 258 (bottom row, left) Poliform; 259 (middle row, left) Valli & Valli; 259 (bottom row, left) Tribù; 260 (top row, centre) Luke Furniture; 262 (top row, left) La Rinascente; 262 (top row, centre) Dorothée Dubois; 262 (top row, right) SAFI; 263 (middle row, right) 3DEOLOGY; 267 (middle row, right), 267 (bottom row, left and right) 3DEOLOGY/Vincent Van Duysen Architects.

We are very grateful to Dedeyne Construct, De Coene and Poliform for their support.